Right to Remember

A Handbook for Education
with Young People
on the Roma Genocide

Written by Ellie Keen

Edited by Rui Gomes

http://www.coe.int/youth/roma

Right to Remember - A Handbook for Education with Young People on the Roma Genocide

The views expressed in this manual do not necessarily reflect the opinions of the Council of Europe.

Copyright of this publication is held by the Council of Europe. No parts of this publication may be reproduced or transmitted for commercial purposes in any form or by any means, electronic (CDRom, Internet, etc.) or mechanical including photocopying, recording or any information storage or retrieval system, without the permission in writing from the Publishing Division (publishing@coe.int), Directorate of Communication of the Council of Europe (copy to the European Youth Centre Budapest, 1-3 Zivatar utca, H-1024 Budapest, Hungary; email: eycb.secretariat@coe.int).

Reproduction of material from this publication is authorised for non-commercial education purposes only and on condition that the source is properly quoted.

All other correspondence concerning this document should be addressed to the Youth Department of the Council of Europe:

> European Youth Centre Strasbourg
> 30, rue Pierre de Coubertin
> F- 67075 Strasbourg Cedex – France
> Email: youth@coe.int

© Council of Europe, 2014

Proofreading: Rachel Appleby

Layout and design: Pampaneo

Photo: Eukalyptus (Pixabay)

Printed in Hungary

ISBN: 978-92-871-7932-6

Acknowledgements

We would like to express our gratitude to all those who contributed to this publication, with their suggestions and feedback, in particular:

- The participants in the consultative meeting held in Strasbourg in December 2013, for their invaluable contribution to making this a useful tool for educators and youth organisations: Gerhard Baumgartner (Austrian initiative for educational materials on Roma Genocide); Nathan Chicheportiche (European Union of Jewish Students); Maryana Borisova, Vicente Rodríguez Fernández, Alexandra Jach, Rebekah Ward (ternYpe, International Roma Youth Network); Angel Ivanov (Forum of European Roma Young People); Zuzana Brodilová (Konexe); Robert Sigel (Bavarian State Center for Civic Education); Simona Vannini (Pestalozzi Programme); Dzafer Buzoli (Docba); Nicolae Radița (Council of Europe Ad hoc Committee of Experts on Roma Issues /CAHROM); Piotr Trojanski (Krakow Pedagogical University); Felicia Waldman (Romanian Delegation to the International Holocaust Remembrance Alliance, Member of the Committee on the Roma Genocide); Alina Onchis (Ruhama Foundation)

- Zara Lavchyan, who acted as a consultant for collecting information for the handbook from different organisations and institutions

- Aurora Ailincăi, Ana Rozanova, Michael Guet (Support Team for the Special Representative of the Secretary General for Roma Issues, Council of Europe)

- Clémentine Trolong-Bailly, Robert Rustem (European Roma and Travellers Forum)

- Nina Kapoor (Youth Department, Council of Europe), for helping to find a title for this handbook

- Mara Georgescu (Youth Department, Council of Europe), for the project coordination.

We have made all possible efforts to trace references of texts and activities to their authors and give them the necessary credits. We apologise for any omissions and will be pleased to correct them in the next edition.

[Preface/Avant-propos]

The youth policy of the Council of Europe aims at providing young people – girls and boys, young women and young men – with equal opportunities and experience which enable them to develop the knowledge, skills and competences to play a full part in all aspects of society. This definition acknowledges that not all young people enjoy the same opportunities, notably because they are the subject of discrimination. The priorities of the Council of Europe youth policy include therefore measures for "preventing and counteracting all forms of racism and discrimination on any ground", ensuring young people's full enjoyment of human rights and human dignity, and encouraging their commitment in this respect. The adoption of the Roma Youth Action Plan as part of the programme of activities of the Council of Europe is a political and practical consequence of the need to secure equality of opportunities in participation of all young people, Roma included.

The Roma youth taking part in the elaboration of the Roma Youth Action Plan identified the *strengthening of Roma youth identity* as the first priority of the plan. The work on identity was perceived by them as necessary, in view of creating an environment where "Roma young people can grow free from discrimination and confident about their identity and future perspectives while appreciating their history, plural cultural backgrounds and affiliations as young people, as Roma, as citizens of their countries and as active Europeans"[1].

The personal need to understand one's past and history is understandably more important in the case of a community, the Roma, whose history is largely ignored and generally side-lined by mainstream history. That Roma young people acknowledge the importance of learning about their history in order to grow up confidently as young Europeans is evidence that identities do not have to be constructed in opposition to other identities or in self-defence. A community that is aware of its history is more likely to look at the future with confidence. More importantly, a sense of history is necessary in order to restore dignity and to empower the victims of massive human rights violations into actors for the struggle of securing human rights and dignity for everyone.

The work on remembrance of the Roma Genocide has been actively pursued by Roma youth organisations and movements, notably through activities commemorating 2 August as International Day of Remembrance of the Roma Holocaust. The Roma Youth Action Plan could not ignore the calls for learning about the Genocide by both Roma and non-Roma youth.

The need for education for remembrance is seen as both a tool for strengthening the identity of the Roma young people and a tool for fighting for human rights and against discrimination. Moreover, the need for these types of educational tools can also be seen in the growing amount of hate speech towards Roma people, much of which refers also to the Genocide! Hate speech and abuse threatens the fundamental values and principles of democracy and human rights and it is unacceptable. The No Hate Speech Movement youth campaign of the Council of Europe has collected numerous examples of hate speech targeting Roma. Combined with the persistence – and sometimes impunity – of racist violence and discrimination, they provide sufficient evidence on why remembrance of the Roma Genocide is so important in Europe today.

This task is particularly difficult for the Council of Europe's youth sector because our tradition of working with non-formal education principles does not pre-dispose us to work on history matters. Other Council of Europe sectors have considerably more expertise and credibility, as attested by the recently published book, *Shared histories for a Europe without dividing lines*. Working on remembrance, however, is more than just history. As practised in human rights education and in education about the Holocaust, remembrance is more than just learning about the past: it is learning from the past so that it is not repeated. Furthermore, it is about restoring a sense of dignity and justice to the victims and to their families and communities.

Education for remembrance is therefore fully pertinent to the work on empowerment of young people and in facilitating the access of vulnerable youth groups to their rights. Involving young people, including Roma youth, in researching, discussing and discovering the meanings of the Roma Genocide before 1945 and today is also a way to involve them as agents and actors in their own understanding of human rights and of history.

This handbook is a self-contained educational resource that does not replace the work of historians; on the contrary, it aims to make history accessible, expose its complexity and link it with the situation today in order to pursue the long-term goal of human rights for all. This handbook is now here to serve both teachers as well as NGOs and youth organisations, to work with young people on the remembrance of the Roma Genocide.

It is based on the principles of human rights education and places remembrance as an aspect of *learning about, through* and *for* human rights. The handbook itself includes educational activities, detailed explanations of how to prepare and run them, as well as commemoration events and information about the Genocide and its relevance to the situation of the Roma people today.

This handbook also takes a clearly anti-racist approach and expresses the need for learning about the past as a necessary step in order never again to reach any kind of situation as the ones during the Second World War. If it is true that "race has been semantically conquered, but remains deeply ingrained in the political imaginaries, structures and practices"[2], young people ought to have opportunities to understand the consequences of racism and their prevalence today so that the eradication of racism can begin. This is certainly a task for education everywhere: in the formal and non-formal settings and additionally taking advantage of informal education.

This is a modest contribution to this process, but one that we hope will inspire others to do better and to do more for the present and the future of human rights in our societies.

---

[1] Roma Youth Action Plan presentation, Council of Europe, 2013
[2] Alana Lentin and Gavan Titley, *The Crisis of Multiculturalism – Racism in a Neoliberal Age*, Zed Books, London, 2011

Table of contents

1 Introduction 11
   1.1 A forgotten genocide 11
   1.2 About the handbook 13

2 The Roma Genocide 17
   2.1 A European genocide 18
   2.3 Resistance 31
   2.4 Historical background 34
   2.5 After the Genocide. 40

3 The Need For Remembrance. 43
   3.1 What is remembrance? 43
   3.2 Why do we need to remember?. 43
   3.3 How should we 'remember'?. 46

4 A Human Rights Concern 49
   4.1 What are human rights?. 49
   4.2 Human rights and the Holocaust 50
   4.3 Human rights and the law 54
   4.4 Genocide 57

5 Advice for Educators. 59
   5.1 Things to bear in mind before you start. 60
   5.2 Planning your activities 62
   5.3 Starting from where the group is. 63
   5.4 Encouraging action 66
   5.5 Facilitation 67

6 Educational Activities 69
   6.1 What happened?. 69
   6.2 Why did it happen? 78
   6.3 Why was it wrong?. 83
   6.4 How does it relate to today?. 86
   6.5 What can we do?. 92

7 The Council of Europe, Education and Remembrance of the Roma Genocide. 99

Appendix 1: Human Rights Documents. 101
   Universal Declaration of Human Rights (abbreviated version). 101
   European Convention on Human Rights (abbreviated version) 102

Appendix 2: Testimonies 103
   Ilona Lendvai – deported with her family to Camp Csillagerőd 103

Anuța Branzan – deported with her family to Transnistria 105
Maria Peter – deported to Auschwitz. 106
Appendix 3: Recognition and Commemorations of the Genocide in European Countries . . 109
Appendix 4: Links to Online Resources 115
General resources on the Roma Genocide 115
General resources on Roma history / culture/ language, etc.. 116
Human rights. 116

A note on terminology

The term 'Roma' is used throughout this publication to refer to Roma, Sinti, Kale and related groups in Europe, including Travellers and the Eastern groups (Dom and Lom). It should be understood to cover the wide diversity of the groups concerned, including persons who identify themselves as Gypsies.

The term 'Rom' is also used to refer to a person of Roma origin.

Both 'Roma' and 'Romani' are used as adjectives: a 'Roma(ni) woman', 'Roma(ni) communities'.

1 Introduction

> In November, 1942, the pogrom against the Jews and Gypsies began, and they were shot on a mass scale in street executions … . It was cold, and the Gypsy women were weeping loudly. They had all their possessions on their backs, including eiderdowns; everything that they had, but all of that was taken away from them later… . They were taken to the station and loaded into goods wagons, which were sealed and taken to stations beyond Chelm, to Sobibor, where they were burnt in the ovens.
>
> *Camp survivor B. Stawska describing the transportation of Romanies to Sobibor (Fickowski, 1989)*

1.1 A forgotten genocide

Much has been written about the importance of Holocaust education. Such work is already supported by numerous handbooks and other educational resources. However, among all these resources, only a very small proportion is directed specifically towards the way the Roma population was targeted for systematic murder. Where Roma victims do deserve a mention, it is generally no more than a side-note: the Roma are seen as one of the "additional groups" that suffered at the time.

> The genocide of the Sinti and Roma was carried out from the same motive of racial mania, with the same premeditation, with the same wish for the systematic and total extermination as the genocide of the Jews. Complete families from the very young to the very old were systematically murdered within the entire sphere of influence of the National Socialists.
>
> *Roman Herzog, Federal President of Germany, 16 March 1997*

The Roma were not an "additional group". They were one of the key groups targeted for complete elimination by the Nazis. By the end of the War, the size of the Roma population was believed to be just 20% - 30% of what it had been at the start. Perhaps 80% had been killed, amounting to at least half a million people.

> Within the [Łódź] ghetto, the Roma were confined to a *Zigeunerlager*, separated from the rest of the ghetto by barbed wire. Living conditions were even more wretched than in the rest of the ghetto. In late 1941, in a few weeks' time approximately 700 Roma – mainly children – died in Łódź of an infectious epidemic disease.
>
> *http://www.romasinti.eu*

The thoroughness with which the Genocide was carried out varied from country to country: in some countries, there were almost no Roma remaining when the War came to a close. In others, where part of the Roma population survived, those left alive would almost certainly have witnessed mass deaths, often of their closest family. They were likely to have spent the war-time years in labour camps, forced exile, or hiding underground. "Surviving" normally meant a state of bare existence, on the edges of starvation or disease, in constant fear for one's life.

The Roma Genocide was wholly European. Across the continent, throughout the period of the Second World War, Roma in mass numbers were vilified, targeted and killed, for nothing more than being Roma. Whole families were rounded up, torn from their homes, herded into camps or segregated areas, threatened, beaten, mutilated, starved; and then, in very significant numbers, deliberately killed off. The victims were parents, grandparents, aunts, uncles and cousins, infants, toddlers and teenagers: no-one was too young or too old.

> When I went in [to the camp hospital], the children cried and asked, 'Uncle, give bread, give sugar' … . For me those were the most difficult moments I experienced in the camp. Not the beating, not the interrogation, but those children.
>
> *Dr Frantisek Janouch, a Czech prisoner employed as a doctor in the Zigeunerlager*

Today, despite the frequent calls to 'remember' the Holocaust, the Roma plight has all but been forgotten. In truth, it has never been fully acknowledged. One indication of that failure is the state of almost total ignorance: among young people in Europe, perhaps the majority are unaware of the terrible crimes and suffering that the Roma people had to endure.

There are important reasons why this lack of attention and lack of balance need to be addressed. Some of the reasons are to do with the historical record and the extreme nature of the crimes against the Roma people; some are to do with the need for *any* past victim to feel that crimes against them have been acknowledged – and remedied; and some are to do with how the majority non-Roma population continues to view and treat representatives of this community today.

The crimes of the past have not been laid to rest for the Roma. They have barely even been recognised and there has never been a common reckoning of their significance and impact for the Roma population, let alone a re-evaluation of the way society behaves towards this minority. In fact, in many ways, the behaviour of the non-Roma population today recalls and repeats some of the patterns which allowed those crimes to happen.

This handbook is an attempt to redress this balance.

> I walked around the camp and tried to keep busy. That was why I walked up to the barbed wire on the crematorium side. I saw a long line of people there, wandering towards the crematorium… . At first I could not understand what I was seeing: there were corpses sprinkled with white lye, and they were all jumbled up. As a child, I could not imagine what they were. Later, when I was about twenty, that scene began coming back to me in nightmares… . As a child, I was completely unaware of how many terrible things I had to look at in the camp.
>
> *Else Baker who was deported to Auschwitz as a child in May 1944. Her mother was half-Roma.*

1.2 About the handbook

This handbook is intended as a self-contained resource for those wishing to promote a deeper understanding and awareness of the Roma Genocide. It has been designed primarily for youth workers in non-formal settings, but it will be useful for anyone working in education, including in the formal sector. The activities provided in the final section are aimed at a target audience of young people from 15 to 30 years old.

The handbook does not provide a complete historical account of the Roma Genocide. We have attempted to base the information on generally accepted existing historical sources and research but these are still thin on the ground, and some may be disputed, or subject to different interpretations. The Roma Genocide is an area which has not yet been as well studied as the Jewish Holocaust: some facts or issues are still controversial, and all are highly sensitive.

Perhaps more importantly, for reasons of space and in order to make the handbook useable and understandable, the picture presented is a simplified one. A large number of facts have had to be left out, particularly those relating to the different practices or circumstances across the region.

The handbook should be seen as offering a general picture, designed to prompt ideas and questions and to stimulate research and action on the part of individual youth groups. We hope that you will encourage those you work with to explore the area further, filling in the details for your country or your region. You can use some of the resources listed in the Appendix at the back.

Outline of chapters

- **Chapter 1, Introduction**

- **Chapter 2, The Roma Genocide**, provides some background to the Genocide for those unfamiliar with the details. Given the space available in a publication such as this, the information is necessarily selective and does not deal with all the various crimes, nor with every aspect of their impact on the people who were victimised. The quotes throughout the text and personal testimonies included at the end (page 103) complete some of the gaps.

- **Chapter 3, The Need for Remembrance**, looks at the purpose – and importance – of 'remembering' the Roma Genocide, not only for the Roma people but also for society as a whole. The questions raised in this section are at least as important as the 'facts' about the Genocide itself: effective work on this theme needs to be more than just a lesson in history.

- **Chapter 4, A Human Rights Perspective**, provides some background on human rights, relating these both to the Genocide and to the way that the Roma community is treated today across the continent of Europe. Human rights are important because they offer a set of common standards for society. Building them into activities with young people will help them to assess the terrible events of the Holocaust according to established universal standards, and will provide important reference points for what is happening today.

> Teaching and learning practices and activities should follow and promote democratic and human rights values and principles.
>
> *Council of Europe Charter on Education for Democratic Citizenship and Human Rights Education*

- **Chapter 5, Advice for Educators**, offers some practical guidelines for educational work on this topic. It outlines an approach to working with young people which will help to raise awareness of the Genocide but should also allow them to see its historical relevance for themselves and for today. Ideally, such work will prompt participants to take the 'lessons' out into the world.

- **Chapter 6, Educational Activities**, includes a selection of activities which can be used with young people to explore issues around the Genocide. These activities are presented in outline form and will be greatly enhanced if they are supplemented with material from preceding sections.

- **Chapter 7** and the **Appendices** include further resources to support the activities, including a few personal testimonies from Roma survivors of the Holocaust, abbreviated versions of key human rights documents, and a number of links to useful online resources.

Although it may be tempting for educators to move straight to the activities, you are strongly encouraged to look through the other sections! These contain information and ideas which will help you in deciding on the most appropriate approach for your group. Most of the ideas can also usefully be shared with participants.

1.3 Terminology

Roma / Gypsy / Traveller

The term 'Gypsy' has traditionally been used by the 'non-Gypsy' population to refer to a number of different communities, including the Roma, Sinti, Kale and related groups in Europe, such as Travellers. Although a very few 'Gypsy' communities do self-identify using this term, in general the meaning of the word is highly derogatory and carries almost entirely negative connotations.

1 Introduction

> The Gypsy question is for us today primarily a racial question. Thus, the national socialist state will basically have to settle the Gypsy question just as it has solved the Jewish question. We have already begun…
>
> *Adam Wurth, Racial Hygiene Research Unit at the Nazi Department of Health*

For this reason, the Council of Europe avoids the use of the term 'Gypsy' and refers to all these groups as 'Roma'. This is the terminology employed throughout the handbook. However, references to 'gypsies' in official documents or in quotations have been retained in order not to alter the (often negative) meaning intended by the authors of these quotes.

The term 'antigypsyism' refers to racism against the Roma (in the above sense). The term is addressed not at Roma, but at the majority and has been included in ECRI's 2011 *General Policy Recommendation (No. 13) on combating anti-Gypsyism and discrimination against the Roma*.

> Antigypsyism is a specific form of racism, an ideology of racial superiority, a form of dehumanisation and of institutional racism […] fuelled by historical discrimination.
>
> *Valeriu Nicolae, former Secretary General of ERGO (European Roma Grassroots Organisation)*

Roma Genocide / Roma Holocaust

The word 'holocaust' is derived from the Greek words *holos* (whole) and *kaustos* (burned) and has been used for many centuries to refer to large-scale massacres of populations. Since the 1960s, 'the Holocaust' has been used to refer to the mass killings of the Nazi era – often restricted to the killings of Jews. This handbook uses the term to cover all victims – including the Roma – who were deliberately targeted and murdered by the Nazi regime or by Nazi collaborators.

The term 'genocide' is a relatively recent one and is used almost interchangeably with 'Holocaust' throughout this handbook. There are various definitions of genocide which differ slightly, but the general sense is given by the 1946 UN General Assembly Resolution 96 (1): "Genocide is a denial of the right of existence of entire human groups, as homicide is the denial of the right to live of individual human beings".

> [the defendants] conducted deliberate and systematic genocide … against the civilian populations of certain occupied territories in order to destroy particular races and classes of people, and national, racial or religious groups, particularly Jews, Poles, Gypsies and others.
>
> *Count 3 of the indictment of Nazi leaders at the Nuremburg Trials*

The international legal definition of the crime of genocide is found in Article II of the 1948 Convention on the Prevention and Punishment of Genocide (see page 57 for the definition).

Some commentators use other Romani terms to refer to the Nazi attempts to eliminate the Roma population – in particular, *Porrajmos* or *Pharrajimos* (devouring or destruction), *Samudaripen* (mass killing) and *Kalí Traš* (black fear). Many Roma groups prefer to use one or other of these terms to refer to the events which took place during the Second World War. However, there is no general agreement even among Roma communities on a single most appropriate term. You should find out which term is preferred by Roma groups in your country or by your own participants.

Girls employed in the Wehrmacht as stenographers, OT workers, conservatory students, and other people leading a solid existence and having worked honestly for long years suddenly found themselves in the concentration camp with their hair cut off, prisoner numbers tattooed on them, and wearing blue-and-white striped uniforms. Yet there was more – the madness kept spreading in further circles. Hundreds of soldiers were brought straight from the front who had not even been aware that they were mixed-blood Gypsies, and they were ordered to take off their uniforms and shipped to the concentration camps only because they possessed 12% or even less Gypsy blood…

From the memoirs of SS-Rottenfuhrer Pery Broad, a functionary of the camp Gestapo at Auschwitz

2 The Roma Genocide

With respect to the extermination of antisocial forms of life, Dr Goebbels is of the opinion that Jews and Gypsies should simply be exterminated.

Otto Thierack, Reichsminister of Justice

It was the wish of the all-powerful Reichsführer Adolf Hitler to have the Gypsies disappear from the face of the earth.

SS Officer Pery Broad, Auschwitz Political Division

We have identified the Roma as totally primitive people of ethnic origin, whose mental retardation renders them incapable of real social adaptation... The Gypsy question can only be resolved when... reproduction of this population of mixed blood is stopped once and for all.

Dr Ritter, Research Institute of Racial Hygiene

All Gypsies should be treated as hereditarily sick; the only solution is elimination. The aim should therefore be the elimination without hesitation of this defective element in the population.

Johannes Behrendt, Office of Racial Hygiene

... additionally to the Jews, normally only the Gypsies belong to impure races in Europe ...

Nuremberg Laws 1935

The final resolution, as formulated by Himmler in his 'Decree for Basic Regulations to Resolve the Gypsy Question as Required by the Nature of Race' of 8 December 1938, meant that preparations were to begin for the complete extermination of the Sinti and Roma.

Auschwitz Memorial Book

2.1 A European genocide

There have been genocides in history and there have been genocides perpetrated by the Europeans. The colonisation of the Americas and of the African continent, as well as other parts of the world, were often characterised by mass elimination of native peoples carried out by European powers. Even after the Holocaust, when the world was supposed to have "learned the lessons", genocides have continued, often with the active assistance or collaboration of European governments.

However, there were features of the Nazi Genocides which distinguished them from many of the previous European genocides. The first was the use of more advanced technologies and a systematic approach both to the rounding up of targeted populations and to their elimination. The use of gas chambers is perhaps the most obvious example, although these existed even before the Second World War.

The second feature was that this was the first mass Genocide carried out within the borders of Europe by various European powers simultaneously; and the target population in every country which participated was the same – or was perceived to be the same. This was a Genocide that was both internal to Europe and was also, in many cases, internal to each country that participated.

This perhaps deserves some explanation. The Holocaust is often treated as a single Genocide, carried out across much of the continent of Europe by the Nazis. In countries other than Germany, responsibility for all the crimes across the region is often laid at the door of the Nazi regime as an "outside power". But while it is true that the initial policy directive was issued by the German government, the countries which took part in the Genocide all co-operated with this policy to varying degrees. Without their co-operation, the Genocide would have been very difficult, if not impossible, to implement.

> On the road to Transnistria we were beaten, [but] beaten less by the Romanian constables. On the other hand, when we passed Bessarabia there everybody beat us. Antonescu hated the Gypsies. He was the one who hated and harmed us. When we arrived there they made fun of us and put us to hard labour, working us like animals. They kept us there for two years without us being spared any suffering.
>
> *Vasile Ioniță, a Romanian Roma*

2 The Roma Genocide

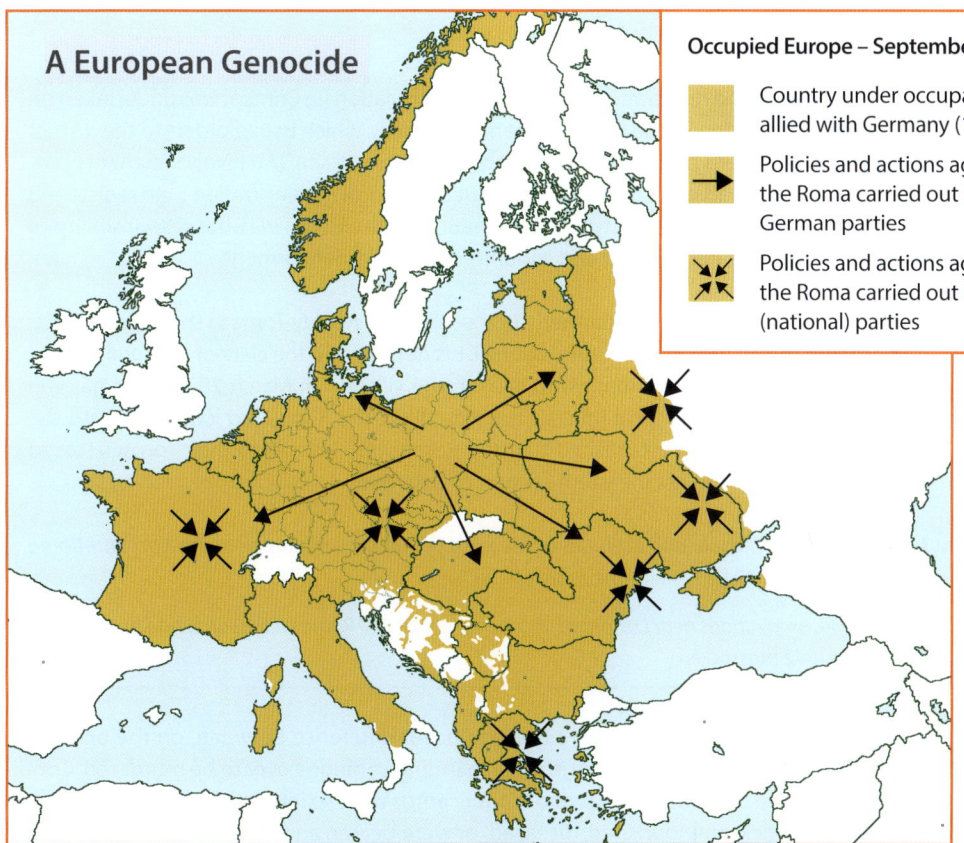

This is a schematic map, reminding us that there were both internal and external contributions to the Genocide in countries across the region. The regions identified are merely illustrative.

The pattern in different countries

In some of the occupied territories or in countries allied with Germany, the actual acts of killing were mostly carried out by German officials. This was particularly true, for example, in Poland, where large numbers of Roma were killed in the Nazi-run death camps. It was also true in other countries such as the Baltic States and former Soviet Union, where the German special troops – the SS Einsatzgruppen – roamed the country rounding up Jews and Roma and shooting them on the spot or gassing them in vans.

However, even in these cases, as the quote on Crimea (below) indicates, the co-operation of local officials was necessary for the identification and rounding-up of victims. This process was likely to be very brutal in itself, and the victims were often then detained under local guard while awaiting murder at the hands of Nazi officials.

> **Roma victims in Crimea**
>
> The identification and registration of the Romani population [in Crimea] was undertaken on the initiative and orders of the field commandant offices, which issued orders to the district headmen, who in turn passed them on to the village headmen. [Archive] documents provide evidence of broad participation on the part of the local administration … in registering and rounding up Roma. The actual extermination of the Roma was the responsibility of detachments of Einsatzgruppe D and subunits of the field gendarmerie ….
>
> In March 1942, the German gendarmerie in the village of Abakly-Toma in the Dzhankoi district ordered the headman of the rural council, his deputy, and the clerk of the rural council to compile a list of the sixty Roma who lived in the village. On March 28, when a gas van came to the village, these local officials helped collect the Roma and load them into the truck. Later, investigators established that the Roma were killed and their corpses tossed out into the open in the northeastern section of Dzhankoi.
>
> *Mikhail Tyaglyy, "The role and attitudes of the local population in Ukraine to the Nazi anti-Roma genocidal politics, 1941-1944 (Crimean case)"*
>
> In May 1944, excavations near Dzhankoi uncovered about 200 Roma victims who had been gassed during the 1942 massacre.

We might ask ourselves whether there is a significant difference between, on the one hand, actually committing murder and, on the other, handing someone over to be murdered. Conditions in many of the detention camps and labour camps were so inhumane that large numbers of Roma became sick, malnourished, diseased, or were beaten and abused, frequently leading to death. Camps of some form were located in almost every occupied or allied country and certain roles were always carried out by local officials.

In certain countries, where the regime was sympathetic to the Nazis, the genocidal policies were implemented more directly by troops or military units local to the country. Such was particularly the case in Hungary after 1944 and in the Czech Republic. It was also true in Croatia and Romania, where the Genocide was almost wholly implemented at the national level. Borders and countries were changing rapidly during that period and sometimes countries allied with Nazi Germany were even engaged in rounding up victims outside their own official territory, for example, Ukrainian Roma within the parts of Transnistria which had been occupied by Romania.

Transnistria itself was used by the Romanian authorities as a place of deportation for huge numbers of Romanian Roma. In 1942, the Romanian leader Ion Antonescu issued an order for "all nomadic Gypsies" to be deported to Transnistria from camps all over the country. This order was later extended to sedentary Roma. In total, over 25,000 Roma were deported to Transnistria where they lived in conditions of extreme hardship, often without food rations. Disease was common and it is estimated that about 11,000 died from hunger, cold or disease.

> *Romanian "researchers" drew on the ideas of Robert Ritter, the intellectual mastermind of the Roma tragedy in Nazi Germany. One such researcher wrote:*
>
> *"Nomadic and semi-nomadic Gypsies shall be interned into forced labour camps. There, their clothes shall be changed, their beards and hair cut, their bodies sterilised […]. Their living expenses shall be covered from their own labour. After one generation, we can get rid of them. In their place, we can put ethnic Romanians from Romania or from abroad, able to do ordered and creative work. The sedentary Gypsy shall be sterilised at home […]. In this way, the peripheries of our villages and towns shall no longer be disease-ridden sites, but an ethnic wall useful for our nation."*
>
> *Ill. 3 (translated from Făcăoaru, Gheorghe (1941) Câteva date în jurul familiei si statului biopolitic, Bu-curești). Quoted in the "Factsheet on Roma Deportations" at http://romafacts.uni-graz.at/*

In Croatia, the Genocide was also at the direction of the national government and implemented by the local population, without the active involvement of the Germans. The fascist Ustaša regime passed a series of racial laws against the Jews and Roma, and Ustaša units conducted brutal campaigns to round up the victims. These included Serbs, Catholics, Muslims and political opponents, as well as the Jews and Roma.

The Ustaša also established a number of concentration camps, the largest of which was Jasenovac where about 26,000 Roma victims are believed to have been murdered.

> **Jasenovac Camp (Croatia)**
>
> The arrests of individual groups of Roma began in July 1941, while mass arrests of Roma all over the Independent State of Croatia were put into practice from 20 May 1942 onwards. They were mostly transported in groups to Jasenovac Camp, with their portable possessions. The accompanying documents did not list their names, only the number of people or freight wagons by which they were transported.
>
> In July 1942, when the number of Roma arriving in the camp was at its highest, they were separated into two groups. The older men, women and children were separated from the younger men and immediately sent to be liquidated in Donja Gradina. The younger men were accommodated in Camp III C, set up in the open on the site of Camp III (Brickworks). Many died of hunger, dehydration, exhaustion and physical abuse. Some Roma were housed in the so-called Gypsy Camp in the village of Uštica, in the abandoned houses of murdered Serbian families … .
>
> Almost no Roma who entered the camp, regardless of age or gender, survived.
>
> *Jasenovac Memorial Site (http://www.jusp-jasenovac.hr)*

The pattern of local collaboration in the Genocide was very diverse and even changed within some countries throughout the years of the War. A few examples have been given above, but there was not one country where the actions against the Roma can be seen as solely the responsibility of an outside power. You are strongly encouraged to investigate with your group the specifics of your region.

A people against itself

We should remember that in addition to the local officials in different countries who played an active role in the Roma Genocide, negative attitudes towards the Roma on the part of the local population was also significant. Even where people did not participate directly, there were relatively few who objected to what was happening. (Activity 5, 'Who contributed?' explores this issue further).

> The German Sinti and Roma are Germans and Germany is their own home country. The Italian Roma and Sinti are Italians and Italy is their own home country. The Spanish Roma have Spain, the Austrian Roma and Sinti have Austria, the Hungarian Roma have Hungary and so on.
>
> *Romani Rose, Roma activist*

A people does not easily turn against itself so violently without a history of antagonism or non-acceptance. The information contained in the following sections outlines some of the worst excesses of the Roma Genocide and briefly sets these against the context of a history of discrimination lasting over centuries.

Of course, it should be noted that "the people" never extends to everyone, and many non-Roma in different European countries did oppose the violent measures against the Roma population. Many even gave them their protection or support. Some of these efforts and individuals are mentioned in Section 2.3.

It is also important to note that the Roma's own resistance throughout the duration of the War was both courageous and persistent. Roma organisations and individuals made regular attempts to protect themselves and others and continued in their efforts to resist the powerful forces which were against them, despite the often fatal consequences of doing so. Some of these are also described in Section 2.3. There are many others.

> Even though I am of Tsigan ['gypsy'] origin, I have lived my whole life a Romanian life, and we identified with the obligations and aspirations of the Romanian people. No blame, no reproach, against any one of these banished from … their beloved country can justify their deportation to a foreign land. I ask you respectfully with all my soul to remember that in the Great War there were *Tsigan* soldiers of *Tsigan* origin and you have seen with how much generosity they gave their blood for our country – because they do not have any other.
>
> *A letter to the Romanian authorities from Dumitru Marin, a Romanian Roma. Marin wrote many letters throughout the war petitioning the Romanian government for the return of members of his extended family who had been deported to Transnistria.*

2.2 Key facts

'Total extermination'

- The Roma were targeted by the Nazi regime in the same way that the Jewish population was: they were supposed to be killed off completely.

- Initially, the official reason given was the Roma's supposed 'criminality' or 'anti-social nature' but there was always an underlying racial element and this became more explicit as the Holocaust reached its climax. By 1938, the 'genetic' basis had become established: someone could be arrested and deported or murdered if just one of their great-grandparents happened to have been Roma.

> The senior SS officer and Chief of Police for the East, Dr Landgraf, in Riga, informed Rosenberg's Reich Commissioner for the East, Lohse, of the inclusion of the Romanies in the 'final solution'. Thereupon, Lohse gave the order, on 24 December 1941, that the Romanies 'should be given the same treatment as the Jews'.
>
> *Benno Müller-Hill, 1988*

- Systematic programmes for moving the Roma into camps or segregated areas existed in every country under Nazi occupation or control. Whole Roma families were taken from their homes and transported *en masse* to almost certain death.

- Hundreds of thousands of European Roma were murdered under the Nazi programme. Precise numbers are unknown as deaths were often not recorded or were not recorded *as* Roma deaths, and many of the records which did exist have been lost or destroyed.

- Most experts agree that at least half a million were killed, amounting to about 70% - 80% of the total Roma population across the region as a whole. Some believe the numbers are much higher, perhaps as high as 1.5 million.

- It was not only the Nazis – or the Germans – who carried out the crimes against the Roma. In Nazi-allied countries, occupied territories or countries under Nazi control, the administration, deportation and often the killing itself were performed under the command of the national government, by local officials. In some countries, almost the whole of the Roma population was killed (see page 19 above for the pattern in different countries, and pages 26 - 30 for statistics on the probable deaths).

> **Conditions of internment in France**
>
> Often the camps were built on a plain or a hillside at the mercy of the elements, as at Lannemezan. They were poorly equipped or even insanitary. Not being designed for this purpose, the premises rapidly became uninhabitable. The beds no longer had mattresses or blankets. The huts were infested by fleas and lice. In Haute-Marne the 'nomads' were interned in a disused fort which no longer had doors, windows or running water. At Mulsanne the huts were roofed with corrugated iron, freezing in winter and stiflingly hot in summer… .
>
> The Roma suffered from the cold because they no longer had any clothes … Having no fuel, the internees at Moisdon-la-Rivière had no option but to burn the floor boards of their huts for heating.
>
> *"Factsheets on Roma History" (Council of Europe). About half of the pre-war Roma population of France, some 13,000 people, were interned in special camps throughout the country.*

Causes of death

- Many Roma were murdered in the gas chambers. The most infamous case was the liquidation of the *Zigeunerlager* – the 'Gypsy Camp' – at Auschwitz-Birkenau. On the night of 2 August 1944, all Romanies living in the camp were herded into the gas chambers and brutally murdered. Almost 3,000 victims were recorded, including men, women, children and the elderly.

> The first attempt to liquidate the *Zigeunerlager* at Auschwitz, was met with unexpected resistance – the Roma fought back with crude weapons – and retreated. A few months later, the SS tried again and this time succeeded in killing all Roma inhabitants.

- Large numbers of Roma were also gassed in other Nazi camps. Roma children were used as 'guinea pigs' in January 1940 for the cyanide gas later used in the gas chambers. 250 Roma children were murdered.

- Tens of thousands of Roma also died as a result of starvation, exhaustion or disease in the concentration camps, ghettos, labour camps or other places where they were deported. Children, the elderly and the disabled, as well as able-bodied young men and women, were barely given enough to eat or drink or keep the cold out; they were held in highly unsanitary conditions, where disease easily took hold, and were not provided with healthcare. On top of this, they were forced to carry out hard labour, and the Roma were often given the very hardest tasks under the worst conditions.

- The majority of Roma victims were probably those murdered in mass execution programmes which were conducted outside the camps by special groups of SS murder squads, known as *Einzatsgruppen*. The murder squads sometimes destroyed whole villages at a time and buried the bodies in mass graves. Very few records were kept and this contributes to the difficulty of knowing how many Roma were killed altogether. So far, about 180 places have been identified where large numbers of Roma were murdered.

> The hunger was the worst thing. Indescribable sanitary conditions. There was no soap and no possibility of washing. When the typhus epidemic broke out, it was impossible to care for the sick because there was no medicine. It was hell. It's hard to imagine anything worse.
>
> The children died first. Day and night they wept and cried for bread … the majority of them died a few days after being born. There was no care, there was no milk or hot water, not to mention powder or diapers. The bigger children, above the age of 10, had to carry stones for the building of the Lagerstrasse. With the hunger that prevailed, hundreds of children died daily…
>
> *Elizabeth Guttenberger, a Roma deported to Auschwitz in 1943*

- Train journeys to the places of deportation and the so-called "death marches" also took thousands of victims. Prisoners had to undergo long journeys often by foot, with little food or water, no health care and no sanitation. Those that could not keep pace – and did not die from exhaustion or starvation – were likely to be shot before they reached their destination.

- The Roma were also the special subjects of "study" and brutal experimentation by the Research Institute of Racial Hygiene, headed by Robert Ritter, and by the infamous Joseph Mengele, who worked at Auschwitz. Some of the "research" included investigating how long Roma could survive on seawater, freezing them, testing new drugs and injecting their eyes with chemicals. Unknown numbers of Roma died either in the course of these experiments or immediately afterwards: survivors of the experiments themselves were normally killed.

> I remember one set of twins in particular: Guido and Ina, aged about four. One day, Mengele took them away … . When they returned, they were in a terrible state: they had been sewn together, back-to-back, like Siamese twins. Their wounds were infected and oozing pus. They screamed day and night. Then their parents – I remember the mother's name was Stella – managed to get some morphine, and they killed the children in order to end their suffering.
>
> *Vera Alexander, a Jewish inmate at Auschwitz who looked after 50 sets of Romani twins*

- It should be remembered that those Roma who were lucky enough to escape death in the war years had lived through an experience that few of today's post-war generation could possibly imagine. In all likelihood, their physical health had been permanently affected by years of malnutrition, disease and severe hardship. However, the consequences of a violent, large scale programme fuelled by prejudice and hatred are bound to be far more than physical: the experience of having witnessed suffering and torment on a massive scale, including that of friends and family, can only have a deep and lasting psychological impact.

> Every evening, the names of the dead were read out … . The camp street in Birkenau was full of corpses lying around in piles, a reality that is hard to describe. At night, when everything was freezing, they loaded the frozen corpses on trucks and took them away. I probably wouldn't have lived through it all if not for my sister, who delivered food.
>
> *Franz Rosenbach, born into a family of assimilated Roma in Austria, deported to Auschwitz in 1943*

Statistics

Research into the Roma Holocaust is relatively recent, and cannot compare with the numerous and substantial studies which have been carried out into the terrible experiences of the Jewish population. Partly for this reason and partly because the records relating to Roma victims are very incomplete, it is difficult to be precise about the number of Roma affected.

The tables on the following pages give some indication of the countries in Europe where significant numbers of Roma were killed over the period of the Second World War. However, if you are using these tables with participants, it is worth noting the following:

1. Unreliability of data

The total number of deaths presented in the tables amounts to less than 300,000. This is lower even than the generally accepted figure of 500,000 Roma deaths, and substantially less than the estimate of many experts on the Roma Holocaust, some of which range as high as 1.5 million. The figures given in the table for different countries are not sufficiently accurate to be used as anything more than a guideline. However, they do present a rough picture of what happened in different regions.

The estimates for the Roma population – both before and after the war – are also uncertain (and disputed). Again, they should be used as a rough guide.

> … the count of half a million Sinti and Roma murdered between 1939 and 1945 is too low to be tenable; for example in the Soviet Union many of the Romani dead were listed under non-specific labels such as *Liquidierungsübrigen* [remainder to be liquidated], 'hangers-on' and 'partisans'… . The final number of the dead Sinti and Roma may never be determined.
>
> *Ulrich König, 1989*

2. Degree of co-operation

The table includes most of the countries which participated in some way with the Nazi policy of targeting the Roma population. Some countries which were allied with or occupied by Germany are not included. Bulgaria and Finland, for example, were notable in not co-operating with the elimination of either the Jewish or the Roma population on their territories. Other countries co-operated more or less willingly but even where the Roma were not formally targeted for elimination – as, for example, in Italy - pre-existing racist attitudes meant that they still became victims.

3. Those countries which fought against the Third Reich and were not occupied did not, of course, send their own Roma populations, nor their Jewish populations, to the Nazi death camps. But, there is nothing to suggest that general attitudes towards the Roma population were substantially different in countries such as the UK, Spain or Sweden. Young people could ask themselves whether the practice in these countries before the War was different enough to suggest that the Genocide would not have been carried out had these countries also been allied with or subject to Nazi control.

There is a great deal of scope for youth groups to add to the body of information which has already been gathered – in particular, by investigating what happened in their locality, and speaking to survivors, eye witnesses, or families of those who perished.

Roma Genocide: deaths across Europe

Country	Pre-Genocide Roma population (estimate)	Holocaust deaths (estimate)	% of population killed (estimate)
Austria	11,200	8,250	73.7%
Belgium	600	500	83.3%
Czech Republic[3]	13,000	6,500	50.0%
Estonia	1,000	1,000	100.0%
France	40,000	15,150	37.9%
Germany	20,000	15,000	75.0%
Greece	?	50	?
Hungary	100,000	28,000	28.0%
Italy	25,000	1,000	4.0%
Latvia	5,000	2,500	50.0%
Lithuania	1,000	1,000	100.0%
Luxembourg	200	200	100.0%
The Netherlands	500	500	100.0%
Poland	50,000	35,000	70.0%
Romania	300,000	36,000	12.0%
Slovakia	80,000	10,000	12.5%
Soviet Union[4]	200,000	35,000	17.5%
Yugoslavia	100,000	90,000	90.0%
Total	**947,500**	**285,650**	**30.1%**

Niewyk, Donald L., Nicosia, Francis R., The Columbia Guide to the Holocaust, Columbia University Press, 2000

3. Protectorate of Bohemia and Moravia

4. 1939 borders

Note: The diagrams on the next page are based on the figures in the table above. They also present only a comparative picture of the fate of the Roma population in the different countries: the number of Roma deaths was almost certainly higher than the diagrams suggest.

Roma deaths - as a percentage of total Roma population

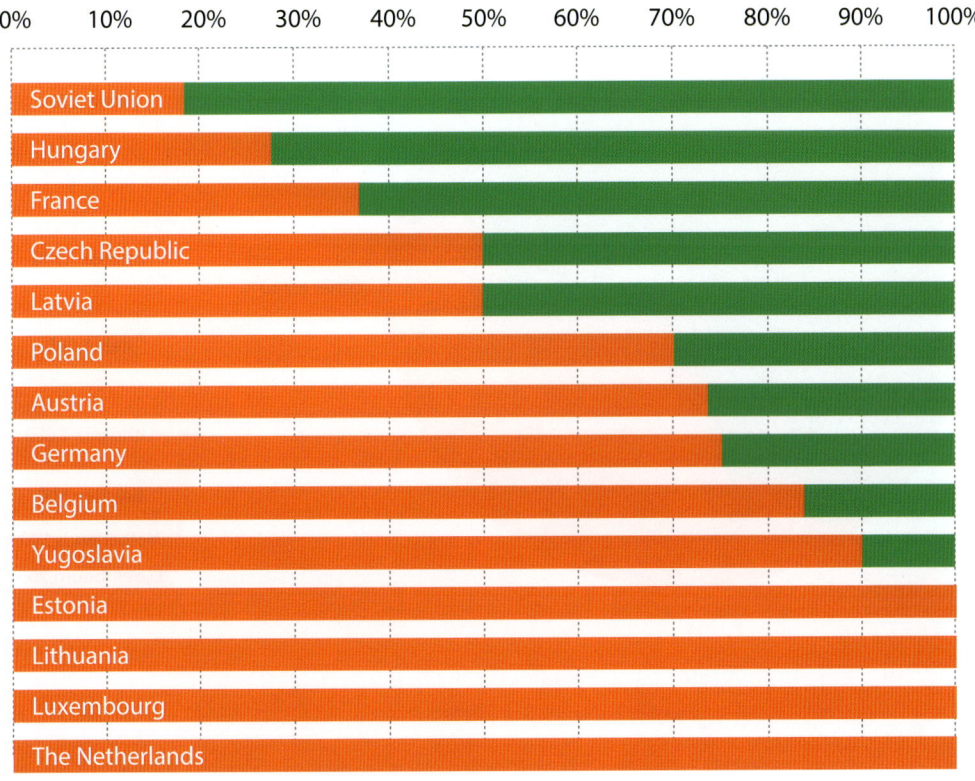

■ Probable deaths, as % of pre-war population
■ Probable survivors, as % of pre-war population

2 The Roma Genocide

Roma deaths: in numbers

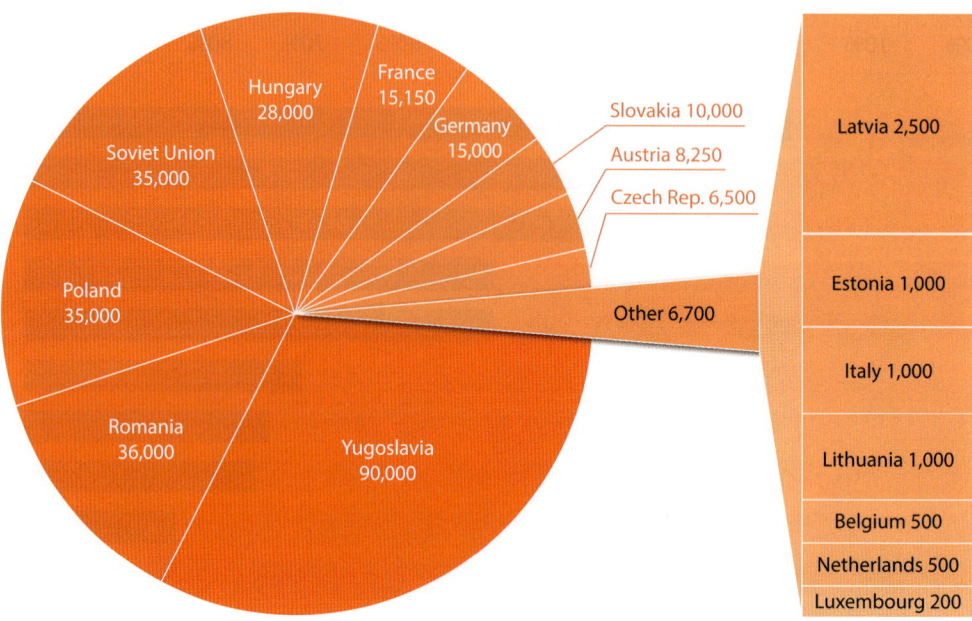

2.3 Resistance

Resisting the Genocide was not easy – for the Roma, above all, but also for any non-Roma who opposed the official policy.

The Roma's own efforts at resistance were continuous throughout the period of the war. They included numerous attempts to avoid captivity themselves or to escape once detained; and they also included efforts to support or save others from death or captivity, often through organised resistance. The most notable of these was in the 'Gypsy Camp' at Auschwitz on the 16 May 1946. When the Nazi SS made their first attempt to liquidate the Camp, the Roma prisoners armed themselves with stones and tools and barricaded themselves in the barracks. The SS were forced to postpone the attempt for another few months. This date, 16 May, is commemorated by several Roma organisations and movements as **Roma Resistance Day**.

> An SS guard told me how much more difficult this special action had been than anything else which had ever been carried out in Auschwitz … . The gypsies, who knew what was in store for them, screamed: fights broke out, shots went off and people were wounded. SS reinforcements arrived when the trucks were only half full. The gypsies even used loaves of bread as missiles. But the SS were too strong, too experienced, too numerous.
>
> *Dazlo Tilany talking about the final 'liquidation' of the 'Gypsy Camp'*

The deported Roma also made various attempts at large-scale organised escapes, some of which were successful. In France, the camp at Arc-et-Senans had to be closed down in September 1943 because so many Roma had managed to escape.

> Iosif Teifel [was] a Rom from Czechoslovakia, who worked clandestinely in the Mukačevo ghetto. Through his work with the partisans, he was able to hide people, provide food aid and carry out resistance activities inside and outside the ghetto during the war.
>
> *USC Shoah Foundation (2013)*

Escapes from Transnistria were also common, as were attempts to appeal on the grounds of deportation. Archives from the period show that many of those who were deported sent numerous letters to the authorities asking for a review of their own case or their family's case. The letters often outlined the important contributions made to Romanian society or to the war effort before the families were deported.

Alfreda Markowska

Alfreda Markowska was a Polish Roma who saw her parents, siblings and members of her community massacred by the Nazis in 1941. She was the only survivor. She managed to avoid arrest and became involved in saving Jewish and Roma children. After hearing news of a massacre, she would travel to the sites to look for survivors. She then took them into hiding, procured false papers and found families or guardians to take care of them. Some she brought up herself.

Alfreda is thought to have saved at least 50 children in this way and in 2005 she was awarded the Commander's Cross with Star of the Order of Polonia Restituta for heroism and exceptional courage.

Support from non-Roma

Various recorded instances of solidarity or support from the non-Roma population have also been recorded, and there are undoubtedly many more which were never documented. Sometimes this support took the form of 'passive' resistance: a delay in executing an order, or a failure to comply completely. Such was the case with some of the local Gendarmerie in Romania who were often unwilling to round up the Roma population when told to do so. A number of local offices sent back the response, "We don't have any Tsigani like this".

Paul Kreber worked for the police in Wuppertal. He refused to carry out deportation orders and often helped the Roma to avoid capture and escape underground. He was awarded the German Federal Cross of Merit in 1988 on the suggestion of the Central Council of German Sinti and Roma.

Other individuals used the opportunities they possessed, and their natural sympathies, to help individual Roma to survive from day to day. Such was even true of some of the guards and staff at the camps or places of detention (see example below).

Mariia Maksymova (née Belous) was born on 1 December 1935, in Nedra, in Baryshivka district of Kyiv region, in the former Soviet Union (now Ukraine) … During the occupation of Nedra, German soldiers arrested Stepan, Mariia's grandfather, and took him to the killing site. It was due to the help of the local villagers and his blacksmith skills that he was left alive.

USC Shoah Foundation (2013)

Of greatest note were those members of the non-Roma population who offered courageous and active support to Roma whose lives were in danger, even when this carried a risk to their own safety. Such, no doubt, was the case with the Polish truck driver who helped Vinzenz Rose to escape from Neckarelz Camp (see pages 34 - 35), and with the police officer who helped Zoni Weisz to avoid deportation. Such, however, was also the case with numerous individuals or families who hid members of the Roma or helped them when they were forced to go underground.

Amidst the brutal climate which prevailed in the years of the Genocide, the actions of such individuals are both remarkable and reassuring. Some Roma lives were saved as a result: that is sufficient result. The fact that human solidarity continued, however, even in these cruel times is perhaps a greater source of optimism for the future.

> I stayed [at the camp hospital] until my departure from Birkenau. I came down with two varieties of typhus … The head nurse was a Polish woman named Janka from Katowice who was around thirty or thirty-five. She was attractive, had dark hair, and was always wearing clean clothes. She looked after me like a mother. She gave me more food and also gave me things that her Polish friends brought her. It was thanks to her care that I survived in the hospital: she saved my life.
>
> *Antonin Absolon, a Roma deported along with his entire family to the Zigeunerlager at Auschwitz*

The Rose family: Roma activists

Anton and Lisetta Rose

Anton and Lisetta were German Roma (Sinti). They were the parents of Oskar and Vinzenz and of a daughter who died in Bergen-Belsen. Before the war, Anton ran a cinema in Darmstadt. He was murdered in Auschwitz and Lisetta died of debilitation at Ravensbruck Concentration Camp. 13 members of the Rose family were victims of the Holocaust.

Oskar Rose

Oskar was able to avoid arrest by the Nazis. While underground, he obtained additional food coupons for his deported family members and enabled Vinzenz to escape from Neckarelz.

Vinzenz Rose

Vinzenz was sent to Auschwitz and then to Neckarelz. He escaped with the help of Oskar and a Polish truck driver. He managed to survive underground until the end of the war.

Romani Rose

Romani is the son of Oskar and has worked actively for Roma rights from an early age and became Chairman of the Central Council of German Sinti and Roma and a member of the executive committee of the International Movement against Discrimination and Racism. He played an important role in obtaining recognition of the Roma Genocide and was influential in obtaining recognition of the German Sinti and Roma as a national minority under the terms of the Council of Europe's *Framework Agreement on the Protection of National Minorities*.

2.4 Historical background

The Roma are known to have arrived in Europe at least 900 years ago, and probably even before that. At least since the 14th Century, there is evidence that they have suffered severe prejudice, discrimination and restrictions of their rights by the majority populations of different European countries. The prejudice and discrimination have been evident both in official policies, and among the general public.

Such negative attitudes, reinforced over hundreds of years and by widespread racism, undoubtedly made it easier for the Nazis – and others – to implement a programme of mass abuse and murder without strong objections of most of the population. Imagine, for example, whether such a programme of mass killing could be announced and carried out today if the

In 1956, Oskar and Vinzenz founded the Association of Racially Persecuted non-Jews. This later became the Association of Sinti of Germany, the first civil rights movement of the Sinti and Roma in Germany.

After Oskar died, Vinzenz continued their joint work to support victims of the Roma Genocide. In 1974 he used his own money to pay for a memorial to the murdered Sinti and Roma on the site of the camp in Auschwitz-Birkenau.

On 4 December 1978, Vinzenz was awarded the German Federal Cross of Merit for his work. He was the first member of the Roma to receive such a high distinction.

Romani has been a leading actor in the struggle to receive recognition for the crimes committed against the Roma during the Holocaust. In 1980, at the age of 30, he took part in a hunger strike at the Dachau camp memorial together with Vinzenz and 10 other German Romanies. The demand was for full "moral rehabilitation".

The week-long hunger strike at the former concentration camp succeeded in bringing the Roma Genocide to public attention. First the Bavarian Government and then the German Chancellor himself acknowledged that the crimes against the Roma at the time of Holocaust were racially founded and amounted to Genocide.

target audience was to consist of people who were regarded "positively", or even neutrally, by society as a whole. Imagine if the targets were declared to be young children with blue eyes or adults with red hair, or comedians – or youth workers. It seems clear that such a programme could almost certainly not be carried out.

The historical discrimination against the Roma is therefore important not only because it is yet one more injustice that should be acknowledged, but also because it can help to explain how such an atmosphere of racism, stigmatisation and prejudice can lead to the possibility of an event like the Holocaust.

Young people need to recognise that racist attitudes can escalate into hatred and abuse. It is such attitudes that make it possible for governments to implement policies which in normal circumstances would be unacceptable.

Discrimination against the Roma throughout Europe: a brief history

Note: "Antigypsy" laws have been passed in nearly every European country, dating almost from the very first migrations of Roma people into Europe. The information below covers only a small selection of such laws in a small selection of countries. European countries which are not mentioned here almost certainly had their own discriminatory laws. Participants should be encouraged to research the history of their own countries.

- From the second half of the 14th century, Roma who arrived in Wallachia and Moldavia (now mostly the territory of **Romania**) were forced into bondage and slavery. This lasted for five centuries. Roma slaves were owned by the Prince, the monasteries or by private individuals. The slaves were not considered legal persons and were classed as the property of their masters.

> Gypsies shall be born only slaves; anyone born of a slave mother shall also become a slave.
>
> *From the code of Wallachia at the beginning of the 19th century*

- The Holy Roman Emperor, Maximilian I (also known as **King of the Germans**) ordered all 'Gypsies' to leave the Empire's territory by Easter 1501. Any Roma remaining after that deadline were declared outlaws, and could be caught and killed by anyone.

- In **France**, Louis XII (1504), Francois I (1539) and Charles IX (1561) expelled 'Gypsies' from the Kingdom. In 1666, Louis XIV decreed that all male 'Gypsies' were to be arrested and sent to the galleys without trial.

- In **Sweden**, the 17th century saw forced sterilisation and deportation of the Roma population. In 1637, the 'Hanging Law' made it legal to kill any Roma found in the kingdom.

- In the **Netherlands** in the 18th century, there were regularly organised actions by the police and military against the Roma. These were known as the 'heidenjachten' (heathen hunts). The last 'heidenjacht' was carried out in 1728. By the time it was over, most of the victims had been murdered, had fled the country, or had given themselves up to the authorities.

- In **England**, under Henry VIII, 'Gypsies' were forbidden to enter the country. Any Roma being found there was deported. In 1554, Queen Mary passed the 'Egyptians Act' which made 'being a Gypsy' punishable by death. In 1714, British Gypsies were shipped to the Caribbean as slaves.

- In 1747, the Bishop of Oviedo, presented a proposal to King Ferdinand VI of **Spain** to deal with the "Gypsy problem", either by exiling them forever from the kingdom or by rounding up and imprisoning the entire 'Gypsy' population. The proposal was carried out on a single day across the country and led to the internment of 10-12,000 people.

> His Majesty now orders that by all means, and in every place, the imprisonment should be sought and executed of those ['Gypsies'] who had remained, reserving no sanctuary whatsoever which they may have taken. The […] magistrates will carry out everything as it is expressed, punctually and completely, as befits a question of this importance.
>
> *From the Order of the Marquis of la Ensenada (Spain, 1749)*

- In 1773, Maria Theresa, Empress of the **Austro-Hungarian Empire**, issued a decree prohibiting marriages between the Roma. The Empress also ordered that all children over the age of 5 should be taken away from their parents and handed over to Hungarian farmers' families.

> On a certain day … soldiers appeared with wagons and took away all children, from the newly-weaned infants to the newly-weds, still wearing their bridal dress, from the Gypsies. The poor people's desperation cannot be described. The parents threw themselves on the ground in front of the soldiers, and clung to the wagons which took away their children. They were pushed away with sticks and rifle butts, and because they could not follow the wagons which held their most precious possessions – their little children – many parents immediately committed suicide.
>
> *Source: Factsheets on Roma History*

- During the 19th century, eugenics and racist theories began to be developed and to be accepted as "scientific fact" by influential writers and by governments. They appeared, to many, to offer a justification for treating people differently who merely "looked different", or who were not regarded as 'native' to a particular country or region.

  Such theories have now been completely discredited, but they played an important role in shaping many of the attitudes and policies towards the Roma population (and others). One influential publication was *The criminal man* by the Italian Cesare Lombroso, published in 1876. Lombroso suggested that "genetic predisposition" was the reason for the alleged criminal acts of the 'Gypsies'.

- In 1927, the First **Czech Republic** passed the 'Law on Wandering Gypsies'. This restricted the movement of Roma, forcing them to apply for identification and for permission to stay overnight.

- In 1926, the fingerprints of all Roma over 14, living in Burgenland (Austria), were taken. From 1928 onwards, the police of Eisenstadt (the new capital of Burgenland) had a so-called "Zigeunerkartothek" ("Gypsy card file"), which included entries of about 8,000 Roma.

1. Sexual intercourse between Gypsies and Germans constitutes an offence of racial disgrace.
2. Gypsies are not allowed to attend the general primary school.
3. Sterilising Gypsies should stop their reproduction.
4. Searchings of houses and individuals has to be conducted regularly.
5. Gypsy huts (a cultural disgrace) are to be pulled down, and the Gypsies lodged in labour camp shacks.
6. In the labour camps, the Gypsies work as closed group.
7. Exercising private professions outside the labour camp is prohibited.
8. Gypsies are not allowed to bear weapons.
9. Voluntary emigration is promoted.

From "The Gypsy Question. Memorandum by the Head of Government of the Province Burgenland" (1938)

Anti-Roma laws and policies in Germany: a brief history (1890 – 1992)

Note: the following table is for use in the activity Dosta! on page 95. For the purposes of the activity, all references to Roma or 'gypsy' have been replaced by 'X'.

1890	A conference is organised in Germany on the "X-scum". The Military is told to control the movements of all Xs.
1909	A policy conference on "The X Question" is held. It is recommended that all Xs be branded with easy identification.
1920	2 academics introduce the notion of "lives unworthy of life," suggesting that Xs should be sterilised and eliminated as a people.
1922	All Xs in German territories (but no other groups) have to be photographed and finger-printed for identification.
1926	A law is passed to control the "X plague".
1927	In Bavaria, special camps are built to imprison Xs. 8,000 Xs are put into these camps.
1928	All Xs are placed under permanent police surveillance. A professor publishes a document suggesting that "it was the Xs who introduced foreign blood into Europe". More camps are built to contain Xs.
1934	Xs are taken for sterilisation by injection and castration, and sent to camps at Dachau and elsewhere. Two laws issued in this year forbid Germans from marrying "Jews, Xs and Negroes".
1938	Between 12 – 18 June, hundreds of Xs throughout Germany and Austria are arrested, beaten, and imprisoned. Xs are the first targeted population to be forbidden from attending school.
1939	The Office of Racial Hygiene issues a statement saying, "All Xs should be treated as hereditarily sick; the only solution is elimination. The aim should therefore be the elimination without hesitation of this defective element in the population".
1940	The first mass genocidal action of the Holocaust: 250 X children are used as guinea pigs to test the cyanide gas crystal at the concentration camp at Buchenwald. Employment of any kind is forbidden to Xs in this same year.
1941	In July the Nazi Final Solution to "kill all Jews, Xs and mental patients" is put into operation. The Holocaust begins. 800 Xs are murdered in one action on the night of 24 December in Crimea.
1944	On 1 August, nearly 3,000 Xs are gassed and incinerated at Auschwitz-Birkenau in one mass action, remembered by survivors as "X-night".
1945	By the end of the war, 70% - 80% of the X population had been annihilated by Nazis. No Xs were called to testify at the Nuremberg Trials; no-one testified on their behalf. No war crime reparations have been paid to the X as a people.

1950	The German government issued a statement saying that they owe nothing to the X people by way of war crime reparations. They continued to deny the existence of the X genocide until 1982.
1992	Germany 'sells' X asylum seekers back to Romania for USD 21 million, and begins shipping them in handcuffs on 1 November. Some X commit suicide rather than go. The German press agency asks Western journalists not to use the word 'deportation' because that word has "uncomfortable historical associations".

Edited version of *A Brief Romani Holocaust Chronology*, by Ian Hancock (full version available at http://www.osi.hu/rpp/holocaust.html)

2.5 After the Genocide

- Roma survivors of the Holocaust were neither immediately acknowledged, nor immediately compensated for the terrible experiences that they had had to endure. No Romanies were asked to testify at the Nuremberg Trials and it took over 30 years for the West German government even to admit that they had been targeted as a people by the Nazi regime. That they did so (in 1979) was largely a result of consistent campaigning on the part of Roma civil society. See the information on Romani Rose on pages 34 - 35 for one important influence.

- In 1979, the German Government at last acknowledged the racial basis for the Roma Genocide, together with the fact that sterilisation of Roma had been part of the 'Final Solution'. A very few Roma survivors became eligible for compensation.

- For former Auschwitz prisoners, compensation was awarded at just EUR 2.50 per day. Of course, even for those able to claim it, the compensation had arrived nearly 35 years after the end of the Genocide. Most of those who would have been eligible were already dead. They had lived through the Holocaust, and lived through a generation of 'remembering' the Holocaust. Their own suffering had been forgotten.

- In 2012, almost 70 years after the end of the war, a memorial to the Roma victims of the Holocaust was finally unveiled in Berlin.

> In 2005, the Hungarian Parliament declared 2 August as Roma and Sinti Genocide Remembrance Day. This was followed by the Polish Parliament in 2011.
>
> The date recalls the liquidation of the Zigeunerlager ('Gypsy Camp') at Auschwitz-Birkenau in 1944. Some other countries mark the date unofficially and many non-governmental organisations now organise remembrance events around this date.

- Other countries which participated in the Roma Genocide have been equally slow to acknowledge the extent of the crimes. In 1997, more than 50 years after the event, Hungary became the first country in Central and Eastern Europe to offer blanket compensation to Roma survivors. There were by this time few remaining.

- The mere fact that there is such widespread ignorance of the Roma suffering during the Holocaust – in every country of Europe – is a clear indication that acknowledgement has been insufficient. The crimes can never be properly 'compensated', the harm can never be remedied. However, the 'forgetting', while other victims are remembered, and while the prejudice and scapegoating continue, only exacerbates the crime.

> At school we did learn about the war but not about the Holocaust – and who would be bothered about what happened to a Gypsy? I was born in Slovakia and moved to Olomouc at 8 months old. I grew up in a separate world from other Czechs. No-one at school was interested in knowing us. I was glad to go to school, but the children called me 'smelly Gypsy' and no one would sit next to me.
>
> *Valeria Bockova, whose husband was the child of an Auschwitz survivor*

> The European Roma and Travellers Forum (ERTF), which has a partnership agreement with the Council of Europe and a special status with this institution, is Europe's largest Roma and Travellers organisation. It brings together Europe's main international Roma NGOs and more than 1,500 national Roma and Travellers organisations from most of the Council of Europe member states. The ERTF is active in the fight against antigypsyism and is committed to the promotion of the official recognition of the Roma Genocide. The ERTF protested against the exclusion of Roma speakers during the UN Holocaust commemoration ceremony on 27 January. The ERTF created a website and an online calendar about international, national and local initiatives organised to commemorate the 70th anniversary of the Roma Genocide. The website also contains links and videos to learn more about this tragic event: http://www.2august.ertf.org.

3 The Need For Remembrance

> … everything possible should be done in the educational sphere to prevent recurrence or denial of the devastating events that have marked this century, namely the Holocaust, genocides and other crimes against humanity, ethnic cleansing and the massive violations of human rights and of the fundamental values to which the Council of Europe is particularly committed.
>
> *Council of Europe Committee of Ministers, Recommendation Rec(2001)15 on history teaching in twenty-first-century Europe*

3.1 What is remembrance?

Remembering is not the same as *remembrance*. Although remembering will always be a part of remembrance, it is primarily a personal matter and often something we cannot avoid, even if we want to. Remembrance, on the other hand, is a structured event with a purpose in mind: it is designed to address not only individuals, but also communities or groups – even society as a whole.

In acts of remembrance, we stop short for a while and focus our minds on an event which happened in the past.

3.2 Why do we need to remember?

There are more than enough examples of abuse today which need to be understood and addressed by the next generation. It is important to be clear about why the Roma Genocide, which took place some 70 years ago, is something that needs to be brought to the attention of society as a whole, and of young people in particular.

Past victims need acknowledgement

The reasons for raising awareness of the Genocide are not difficult to see when we consider the nature and scale of the crimes, and put ourselves in the position of the victims. The 'thought experiment' on the next page places the reader in the position of one whose family has experienced gross abuse and a gross injustice. It reminds us that the trauma of our parents is often something that succeeding generations have to carry, and will not forget. It emphasises the entirely human need for past crimes to receive acknowledgement, not only because injustice is painful in itself, but also because a past injustice often affects our current possibilities.

A Thought Experiment

What's in a name?

Imagine how you would feel if sometime in the not-too-distant past, the whole of your family had been violently abused, and most had lost their lives as a result. Imagine that the abuse had been not just unwarranted – you had done nothing wrong – but very deliberate and intended to harm. Imagine it had all happened … just because of your *name*!

The harm was not the act of an individual: it was the act of many individuals. A few directly carried out the crime: pulled the trigger or wielded the weapons used to threaten or mutilate; a few more kept you under control and stopped you from escaping. And many, many more just looked away, doing nothing while it happened. After all, your family had a *Name*. The name was bad: anyone with that name was bad.

Imagine that one member of the family managed to survive: a child, who saw her siblings, parents, grandparents and other close relatives perish. She watched while her baby sister, aunts and uncles slowly starved to death because food was withheld; while cousins had the life beaten out of them by large men wearing uniform; while older brothers, mother, father, and grandparents were led away at gunpoint, never to be seen again.

Aged 14, the miraculous survivor was allowed to return to the "home" from which she and her family had been uprooted not too many years before, but the home had been almost destroyed and the possessions looted. The teenager was unschooled, traumatised by her experience, and quite without support.

Far from recognising how the child had suffered, far from returning even the possessions which her family had owned, and very far from looking inwards at the role of those who had not stepped in to prevent the crime from happening, the child continued to be victimised. She still, after all, had that name.

That *Name*: the name which others automatically assumed made people into dirty criminals. No-one stopped to wonder why; in fact, no-one had *ever* stopped to wonder why. For centuries it had been "common knowledge" that a single name was quite enough to make you bad. The teenager was bound to be no different. The memories would not go away. The child became a woman and then brought children of her own into the world.

How would she cope with motherhood, and how could she rebuild a life while still surrounded by those memories and still surrounded by the hatred and contempt of those around her? How would her children cope with a mother who had had such hardship and such pain inflicted upon her? How would *their* children make their way in the world when even to this day they were perceived by others to be no more than a *name*?

That name. *Your* name.

How would you cope, if it had been your grandmother? Would the past be past, or would you need the present to acknowledge it?

This text is used to support the activity on page 82.

The thought experiment is not really fictional. It applies, in essence, to large numbers of Roma families living in Europe today, particularly in those countries which were under occupation or Nazi control. In those countries, at least, there is barely a Roma family living today whose parents or grandparents were not touched directly by the Holocaust. For the very few who were fortunate enough to escape direct capture, still, daily life would have been shaped by the awareness that most of those who carried the same 'name' were being threatened, abused and even murdered for that fact alone. Imagine the fear of being next on the list.

> … the fear, always the fear. The children grew up with it. That is why they still turn round when they walk the streets today. Do you understand? They turn round. Only someone who is afraid turns round!
>
> *Ceija Stojka, Roma painter, musician and Holocaust survivor*

> The fascists destroyed our lives, so that even today we are unable to forget. Today we wander through the whole of Europe, searching for what the fascists took from us. Among us there are children who have Romani mothers and German fathers – children whose mothers were raped and came into the world that way, children like J.S. and A. who wander with us as Roma and not as Germans. They are also seeking a place where they can stay and lead meaningful, dignified lives.
>
> *Sefedin Jonuz, a Roma who survived the war as a child in Skopje*

The name of 'gypsy'

Of course, the name in this case is the name not of a real family, but a diverse ethnic identity. The treatment was no more acceptable for that; it was no more justifiable, and no less terrifying. Indeed, the identification of Roma for the purposes of the Nazi "programme" was often actually carried out on the basis of family names: if someone had a 'Gypsy' surname, they were an immediate target.

Society needs remembrance

> The Czech Republic, Hungary, Romania and Slovakia have never thoroughly come to grips with their shared responsibility for the crimes committed against Jewish and Roma people.
>
> *Romani Rose, Romani activist and Chairman of the Central Council of German Sinti and Roma (2011)*

Society needs to 'remember' its own history in order to learn from the past and not repeat mistakes or crimes for which it may have been responsible. Remembrance, when done properly, can serve as a warning signal: it can show us how human action or inaction, bigotry, racism, intolerance, and other relatively common attitudes are unacceptable in themselves; and how they can lead, under certain circumstances, to events which are truly terrible.

This task is all the more important when a tragedy on the scale of the Holocaust has come about as a result of the actions of one sector of society against another. That part of society which bore some responsibility needs to look inside itself: it needs to inspect and understand the causes of the tragedy, to remedy, as far as possible, the harm, and then to review the current ways in which it interacts with those who were previously victimised. Nothing in the present should resemble the errors which led to the past.

However, society, of course, includes the Roma community as well: the failure to recognise this fact was part of what lay behind the Genocide. This raises another important purpose of remembrance for society, understood this time as including the *whole* of society. In other societies where communities have been oppressed, for whatever reason, some form of reconciliation has been helpful for both oppressors and oppressed in moving on. Perhaps some recognition of the centuries-long oppression of the Roma, culminating in the Genocide, might help heal past wounds and help the European countries to build a better common future.

3.3 How should we 'remember'?

> All who have taken seriously the admonition 'Never Again' must ask ourselves – as we observe the horrors around us in the world – if we have used that phrase as a beginning or as an end to our moral concern.
>
> *Harold Zinn, historian*

Official remembrance – as organised by governments – can often be an empty event. Indeed, it can sometimes be worse than empty, serving only to shore up a false sense of benevolence or solidarity among those who display no solidarity on any other day towards the groups that matter. If there is a single message that remembering the Roma Genocide should send, it is that empathy and solidarity towards the Roma were sadly lacking while the Genocide was happening; and although the acts of anti-solidarity today are less extreme, they still exist.

There is little to be gained for either Roma people or society if we 'remember' their suffering on 2 August every year, and then forget again for every other day. Remembrance of the Roma Genocide must be more than a single symbolic event.

Acknowledging the wrong

A human response to the pain or suffering of others is to acknowledge the suffering and try to remedy any continuing damage, and a humane society will want to do this. For survivors of the Holocaust, for the families of survivors and for the families of those who perished, the very least society can do is not forget. This becomes even more important when society itself has been in part responsible for the damage done.

An official remembrance event can offer support to those who have been affected by a terrible past crime if it is done correctly and with sensitivity. It is true that the damage done to individuals and to the Roma as a people can never be erased; however, by recognising the pain and condemning the actions which caused it, society can provide some solace, some reassurance that such actions will not be repeated. Remembrance can help in this way to give a sense of closure to victims, and to enable them to move on from the past.

> After the war no-one spoke about it. There were no memorials. I only knew what had happened through my father. If my father hadn't told me I would never have known – everyone carried on as normal. Dad told us all about his family, how much they had loved each other. He wanted us eight children all to love each other as they had.
>
> *Wilem Bock, a Roma whose father survived Auschwitz*

Involving and including Roma communities

Although remembrance of the Roma Genocide has important messages for the non-Roma community, for remembrance events with a public face, the need for Roma communities to become involved and even to set the agenda is paramount. 'Society' must not take ownership of remembrance events – and nor, ideally, should non-Roma youth groups, however well-intentioned they may be in organising such events. Wherever possible, such events should be led by those to whom the tragedy belonged – the Roma people.

In general, and in consultation with Roma communities, the message for remembrance events, and for the days between them, should try to include the following elements:

- **Acknowledgement of what happened:** a clear statement about the scale of the crime and its impact on individuals

- **Condemnation of the events and of those responsible**, including an understanding that those who stood by also played a role in the events

- **The intention to remedy any remaining harm**. Ideally, this should include specific proposals, whether from official structures or individuals, or from the non-Roma population.

- **The desire to turn a new page**. This involves acknowledging the injustices faced by Roma communities today. Until the racism and discrimination which permeate every European society today – up to the highest levels of government – are eradicated, the Roma will not be justified in believing that their tragedy is really remembered.

> Everybody here knows that Jewish and Polish were killed in the war, but nobody ever says anything about the Roma who were murdered.... In Plaszów there is a plaque remembering the Jews and Polish people who died there – but it doesn't mention the Roma!
>
> *Krystyna, a Polish Roma. As a child, Krystyna and her grandmother were the only survivors from their family, of a Nazi massacre in their village. She survived several years in hiding and then in the Plaszów concentration camp in Kraków. Despite all her suffering, Krystyna only received compensation two years ago. From* http://www.annakari.com/portfolio/holocaust.html

4 A Human Rights Concern

> The Holocaust is regarded as a paradigm for every kind of human rights violation and crime against humanity; all victims are taken into consideration.
>
> *Council of Europe 'Day of Remembrance of the Holocaust and for the Prevention of Crimes against Humanity'*

4.1 What are human rights?

Key facts

- Human rights are internationally agreed standards, based on a set of universal values which have been agreed by every government around the world.

- Human rights are based on the idea that all human beings are worthy of respect and that no-one should have to suffer to such a degree that they are made to feel *less than human*. All human beings are *equal* in this respect; their *dignity* should be treated as a fundamental value.

- Human rights have been embodied in international law, creating obligations for governments around the world. Governments have a duty to ensure that the basic needs of every individual are met – including the need for personal dignity.

- The system of international human rights law was established immediately after the Second World War, and partly as a response to the crimes of the Holocaust. The first human rights documents were drawn up by the United Nations. Regional treaties followed, including treaties at European level.

- Human rights do not ensure a life of luxury, free from all harm or hurt. They provide a baseline, a set of *minimum standards* which define what is required for people to lead a life of dignity.

- Most human rights can be *restricted* under certain circumstances if this is necessary in order to protect the rights of others – or is necessary for society as a whole. Some human rights, for example, the right to life and the right to be free from inhuman and degrading treatment, can never be restricted.

4.2 Human rights and the Holocaust

Speaking of human rights abuses in connection with the Holocaust sometimes seems to understate the horrific nature and extent of that event. After all, human rights abuses happen every day; the Holocaust does not.

In fact, using human rights within remembrance education can add a number of useful dimensions, and it certainly need not "minimise" the nature of the crimes. The Holocaust was a violation of *all* human rights against huge numbers of people – arbitrarily selected, and entirely innocent.

1. Human rights help to identify and classify the different violations

Human rights cover a number of different human concerns and basic needs, for example, the need to have your private life and family life respected, the need for physical security and good health, the need for fair and dignified treatment, for personal autonomy, and so on. Applying the different rights to the crimes committed while the Genocide was happening helps to illustrate the breadth and depth of the injustices.

It was not only 'killing' that was wrong: the list of acts which should not ever have been carried out extends over almost every aspect of the lives of those who were made victims.

So, yes, it is true that human rights abuses happen every day, but it is not every day that every member of a particular minority has to endure comprehensive violation of almost every human right – including the right to life.

Some examples of human rights violations during the Holocaust:

Violation of the right to life: death in the gas chambers, starvation and disease in places of exile (including in the concentration camps), shootings by SS Einsatzgruppen, and murder or preventable death by any other form.

Torture, inhuman and degrading treatment: beatings, harsh medical experiments, forced sterilisation, severe humiliation and degradation – including the conditions in labour camps – and failure to provide adequate food and water or proper sanitation.

Freedom from slavery and forced labour: all Roma prisoners, from young children to elderly pensioners, were forced to work long hours, in unhealthy and degrading conditions, for no pay. Other labour rights, such as the right to free association and collective bargaining, were also ignored.

Discrimination: the different (and inhuman) treatment accorded to individuals simply because they were Roma were all examples of discrimination. Children, women, the disabled, sick and elderly were not given any provision for their specific needs.

Violation of the right to liberty: confinement in camps, prisons, ghettos, segregated regions, and so on.

Right to fair trial and the presumption of innocence: there were no trials to assess the 'guilt' of members of the Roma population; all were 'guilty' merely because they were Roma.

Right to private life, family life and home: families were split up, people were removed from their homes, and every element of privacy and dignity was violated.

Right to adequate healthcare: sickness, disease, and malnutrition were all inflicted on huge numbers of Roma as a result of the conditions they were forced to live in. Almost no medical care was provided.

Right to property: all Roma property was confiscated – and never returned. In many cases, when Roma tried to return to their homes after the war, they found their houses had been destroyed, and their possessions looted. No attempts were made to return them.

Right to effective remedy: even after the war ended, the Roma were given no compensation for crimes committed against them. The crimes were not even acknowledged for many years afterwards.

2. Human rights establish an objective standard

> All human beings are born free and equal in dignity and rights. They are endowed with reason and conscience and should act towards one another in a spirit of brotherhood.
>
> *Article 1, Universal Declaration of Human Rights*

Human rights provide an internationally agreed standard, according to which the many different crimes carried out against the Roma can be assessed. Because these standards are not, in general, disputed, they offer a more "objective" measurement of what was wrong, and *why* it was wrong. Today, with the establishment of an international system which offers protections under the law for human rights, at least in theory, such treatment would be illegal under international law.

3. Human rights provide a set of common moral values

Human rights have been accepted, theoretically at least, by every government around the world because they embody certain values which are so commonly held that no government is prepared to deny them publicly. Appealing to such values as fairness, justice, liberty, autonomy, dignity and equality (or non-discrimination) is a powerful way of making the moral argument about the injustices that the Roma have had to suffer, and continue to suffer. Unwrapping some of the 'moral crimes' by applying these standards can help to show that what was done to the Roma was at the extreme end of the moral scale.

> **Unwrapping the moral crimes**
>
> Consider the following acts of murder: each is "bad" in itself, and one that no society should allow. The Holocaust was a time when all these acts were carried out at once against the Roma community.
>
> - Murder – wilfully taking life
>
> - Murder applied in a slow and brutal fashion, so that the victims know they are to die, and know all members of their family are likely to die
>
> - Murder of people entirely innocent of any crime, committed only on the basis of an arbitrary selection (according to ethnic group)
>
> - Widespread, wholesale murder, so that anyone belonging to that ethnic group is likely to be a victim, and will live in fear of being "found"
>
> - Such murder officially sanctioned by the State and carried out by people in positions of power and authority
>
> - Murder which is witnessed and even facilitated by the majority of the population: few stepped in to help; almost none complained
>
> - Murder which goes unpunished, even unacknowledged, afterwards, and with no attempt at compensation offered
>
> - Murder which is unacknowledged (and not compensated for) even while other almost identical crimes, against the Jews, for example, are acknowledged
>
> - Continuing prejudice and scapegoating of members of the same minority, on the same arbitrary grounds, even after such crimes have been brought to light

4. Human rights connect the Genocide with past abuses

> See Section 2.4 for some of the examples of historical discrimination against the Roma which existed in different European countries.

Human rights can help to identify the patterns of thought and behaviour towards the Roma which most societies practised long before the Holocaust, and which led to the terrible crimes of that time. They can help us to see that the anti-Roma prejudices which existed over many centuries were not only unfair and wrong in themselves, but also led to a state of affairs where mistreating people simply because they were Roma became regarded as "normal", and "acceptable".

Human rights should not be seen as a yes-or-no, black-or-white affair, where certain behaviour is and then suddenly isn't a violation – even if this may be the case in the strictly legal sense. Human rights abuses lie on a spectrum of ill-treatment where some instances may be worse than others, perhaps because the impact on the individual is worse, or because the suffering was deliberate, rather than being a result of inattention.

It is almost invariably the case that the worst instances of human rights violations will have emerged gradually from behaviour or treatment which was increasingly abusive or disrespectful. The Holocaust did not emerge out of nothing, and those who perpetrated the crimes against the Roma were, in the vast majority of cases, "normal" people. There were, after all, too many who participated in some way to class them all as abnormally "evil". It can help to explain – though never to excuse – the abnormal behaviour of the Holocaust if we look at the attitudes which slowly became "normalised" in the years preceding it.

"Normalising" negative attitudes

If the State passed a law which ordered the 'elimination' of all musicians or painters or journalists, or everyone with brown eyes, or anyone overweight, there would be a public outcry. If, however, for many decades before – or longer – there had been stories in the news about the evil nature of one of these groups, and if that belief had become accepted by society, then slowly depriving the group of more and more rights might well come to be regarded as acceptable.

- Why do European societies, even today, "accept" the sterilisation of Roma women?
- Why do they allow deportations of Roma immigrants?
- Why do they keep Roma children out of "normal" schools?
- Why is the destruction of Roma homes and Roma communities regarded as acceptable?
- Are other minorities treated in the same way as the Roma?

How do you think most people in your country would react if the State passed laws restricting Roma people to particular regions or confining their movements and activities – as happened both before and during the Roma Genocide? How would people today react to placing the Roma in 'camps'?

---

5. Human rights relate the Genocide to contemporary events

In a similar way, by comparing the human rights concerns which preceded the worst years of the Holocaust with those which exist today, we can spot patterns and similarities with the past. This is particularly important in remembrance education, not only because *any* similarities in treatment are an offence and an abuse towards the Roma, but also because they may well be a precursor to even worse treatment.

Discrimination and prejudice against Roma people throughout Europe today is increasing. Blanket condemnation, racism and scapegoating are common themes – from politicians, other public figures and the media. With every statement and with every failure to condemn it, the scapegoating and prejudice within society is reinforced: attitudes are strengthened, sanctioned, and "normalised".

The information on the next page illustrates the extent to which Roma communities are disadvantaged and discriminated against even today. The information offers only a general picture: in some countries the situation is worse. There have also been numerous cases at the European Court of Human Rights which have found extreme violations of other rights not mentioned in the table.

> The stigmatizing rhetoric has to stop. Serious steps must be taken to counter discrimination of Roma, not least in their home countries.
>
> *Thomas Hammarberg, former Commissioner for Human Rights of the Council of Europe*

4.3 Human rights and the law

Human rights have been incorporated into various legal systems, creating obligations for governments at a number of levels. Key human rights instruments, together with some of the rights they cover, are shown in the diagram on page 56.

Human rights at international level

The United Nations (UN) has developed a number of human rights treaties which define government obligations with respect to individuals. The most important are:

- The UN Declaration of Human Rights (UDHR). The UDHR was drawn up in 1948, immediately after the Second World War. It has been accepted by every government around the world and sets out the basic rights and fundamental principles to be found in every successive human rights treaty.

- The International Covenant on Civil and Political Rights (ICCPR) was adopted by the UN General Assembly in 1966. It expands many of the rights set out in the UDHR, as illustrated by the diagram on page 56.

- The International Covenant on Economic, Social and Cultural Rights (ICESCR) was adopted by the UN General Assembly at the same time as the ICCPR. It covers the remaining rights in the UDHR, as shown in the diagram.

Discrimination: The situation of Roma in 11 EU Member States

This information is taken from the Fundamental Rights Agency (FRA) Roma pilot survey and the UNDP / World Bank / European Commission regional Roma survey carried out in 2011. The countries included in the survey were: Bulgaria, the Czech Republic, France, Greece, Italy, Hungary, Poland, Portugal, Romania, Slovakia, and Spain.

Education:
- On average, only one out of two Roma children surveyed attend pre-school or kindergarten
- During compulsory school age, with the exception of Bulgaria, Greece and Romania, 9 out of 10 Roma children aged 7 to 15 are reported to be in school
- Participation in education drops considerably after compulsory school: only 15% of young Roma adults surveyed complete upper-secondary general or vocational education.

Health:
- One out of three Roma respondents aged 35 to 54 report health problems limiting their daily activities
- On average, about 20% of Roma respondents are not covered by medical insurance or do not know if they are covered.

Employment:
- On average, fewer than one out of three Roma are reported to be in paid employment
- One out of three Roma respondents said that they are unemployed
- Others said that they are homemakers, retired, not able to work or are self-employed.

Housing:
- On average, in the Roma households surveyed, more than two people live in one room
- About 45% of the Roma live in households that lack at least one of the following basic housing amenities: indoor kitchen, indoor toilet, indoor shower or bath and electricity.

Poverty:
- On average, about 90% of the Roma surveyed live in households with an equivalised income below national poverty lines
- On average, around 40% of Roma live in households where somebody had to go to bed hungry at least once in the last month since they could not afford to buy food.

Discrimination and rights awareness:
- About half of the Roma surveyed said that they have experienced discrimination in the past 12 months because of their ethnic background
- Around 40% of the Roma surveyed are aware of laws forbidding discrimination against ethnic minority people when applying for a job.

Source: http://fra.europa.eu/sites/default/files/fra_uploads/2099-FRA-2012-Roma-at-a-glance_EN.pdf

4 A Human Rights Concern

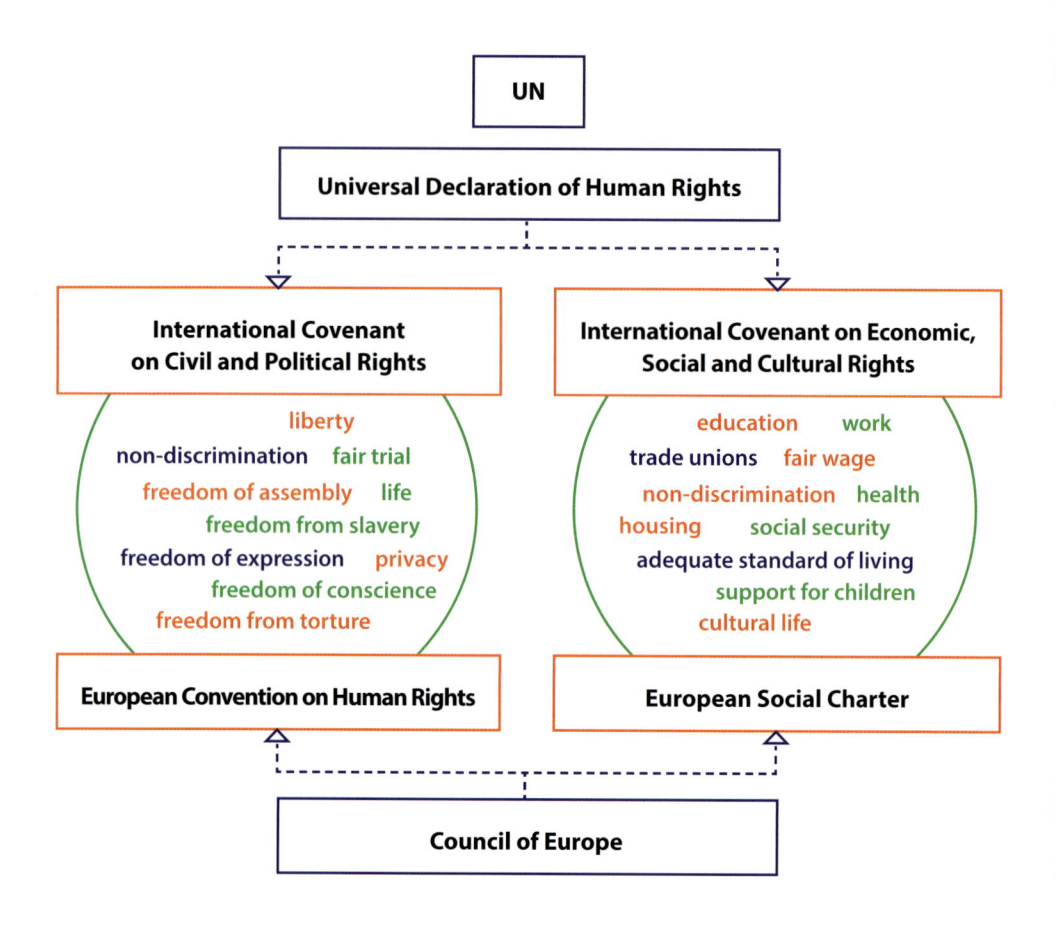

```
                            ┌──────┐
                            │  UN  │
                            └──────┘
                                │
                ┌───────────────────────────────┐
                │ Universal Declaration of       │
                │ Human Rights                   │
                └───────────────────────────────┘
```

International Covenant on Civil and Political Rights

liberty
non-discrimination   fair trial
freedom of assembly   life
freedom from slavery
freedom of expression   privacy
freedom of conscience
freedom from torture

International Covenant on Economic, Social and Cultural Rights

education   work
trade unions   fair wage
non-discrimination   health
housing   social security
adequate standard of living
support for children
cultural life

European Convention on Human Rights

European Social Charter

Council of Europe

All European governments have agreed to respect, protect and fulfil the rights contained in the International Bill of Rights. They have also signed up to various other international human rights treaties, including the UN Convention on the Rights of the Child.

A full summary of rights in the UDHR can be found in the Appendix (page 101).

Human rights at regional level:

The European human rights framework was created, and is monitored, by the Council of Europe, and to a lesser extent by the European Union.

The two key treaties at European level divide the rights in the UDHR in a similar way to the two International Covenants mentioned above, although the European treaties were adopted earlier.

- The European Convention on Human Rights (ECHR) was adopted in 1953 and contains nearly the same rights as those in the ICCPR. The European Court of Human Rights was established in 1959 to oversee Council of Europe member states' observance of the Convention. A summary of the rights in the ECHR can be found on page 102.

- The European Social Charter was adopted in 1961 and contains almost identical rights to those found in the ICESCR. Rights protected by the Social Charter cannot be taken to the European Court. These rights are monitored by a Committee which considers reports submitted by the government (and sometimes other actors, such as NGOs).

Human rights at national level

Many countries also have human rights protections built into their own national legislation. Where this is the case, potential human rights violations can be heard in national courts.

4.4 Genocide

In addition to human rights treaties, which concentrate on the rights of individuals, the United Nations has also adopted a treaty which bans genocide, in other words, the deliberate attempt to "destroy, in whole or in part, a national, ethnical, racial or religious group". This treaty was adopted in 1948 and has been ratified by 144 states.

The UN Convention on the Prevention and Punishment of the Crime of Genocide

Article I: The Contracting Parties confirm that genocide, whether committed in time of peace or in time of war, is a crime under international law which they undertake to prevent and to punish.

Article II: In the present Convention, genocide means any of the following acts committed with intent to destroy, in whole or in part, a national, ethnical, racial or religious group, as such:

(a) Killing members of the group;

(b) Causing serious bodily or mental harm to members of the group;

(c) Deliberately inflicting on the group conditions of life calculated to bring about its physical destruction in whole or in part;

(d) Imposing measures intended to prevent births within the group;

(e) Forcibly transferring children of the group to another group.

5 Advice for Educators

> We wanted to raise awareness about the Porajmos among poor Roma communities and we wanted to spread information about the pig farm on the site of the former WW2 Roma death camp in Lety u Písku. This history is not part of the normal curriculum so there is no public pressure to demolish the pig farm in Lety. 99% of Roma do not know their own history, they don't know what happened in Lety or about the existence of the pig farm.
>
> We do this community education at times of emergency and crisis in communities targeted by anti-Roma riots, marches, or hateful demonstrations. We want to provide a historical background for members of the targeted communities so that they can understand better their current experience.
>
> *Miroslav Brož, Konexe (Czech Republic)*

This chapter includes general recommendations to support the sample educational activities in Chapter 6 (page 69 onwards). These recommendations will also be useful if your group intends to organise actions or events designed to reach a wider public. You will find suggestions for an action-based activity on page 94.

The activities themselves are presented in relatively brief form, without substantial methodological recommendations. If you are unfamiliar with interactive and user-led learning methods, you are advised to take a look at some of the methodological advice in Chapter 1 of *Compass* – the Council of Europe manual for human rights education with young people. This is available online at http://www.coe.int/compass. All the activities are based on the general approaches of human rights education. The information below contains considerations on planning and facilitation which are more particular to specific issues which might arise in connection with the topic, for example, how to meet the different needs of Roma and non-Roma participants.

> 2 August 2010 was the first time in my life that I visited the concentration camp of Auschwitz-Birkenau. I was participating in an event organised by TernYpe-International Roma Youth Network. On that day, my overall comprehension of the past and future of Roma people in Europe changed completely.
>
> *Vicente Rodriguez Fernandez, a Roma, founder of the youth organisation Yag Bari*

5.1 Things to bear in mind before you start

Ten tips

1. Although there are certain basic facts about the Roma Genocide which need to be understood by your group, the importance of remembrance education lies more in how they *process* this information, and how this is likely to affect their behaviour afterwards.

   » Do not be afraid to give time to "sitting and thinking", and try to encourage participants to share concerns or difficulties if they wish to do so.

2. Try not to limit the time you devote to the topic because it appears to be too "narrow": these sessions can also contribute to the understanding of numerous other issues, particularly those relating to discrimination, human rights, and citizenship.

   » *Remember that the Roma Genocide is an important theme in itself, but it can also be useful in meeting other objectives for the group.*

3. Any work on this topic will be improved if it also connects the historical lessons to the present day, and in particular, to young people's own experience.

   » *Try to make the links both forwards and backwards and do not view these sessions as merely a "lesson in history".*

4. Adapt the activities, where necessary, to fit the needs of your group. If the activities do not fit, use the information presented throughout the handbook and the questions at the start of each group of activities to begin a process of reflection, either with the group or on your own before the session. Then design your own activity!

   » *Do not stick rigidly to the activities as they are set out!*

5. Remember that the sessions will be more interesting and "real" if you sometimes take the learning out into the real world. For example, if you have the possibility to speak to survivors, or the families of survivors, this will greatly add to the interest and value of the work.

   » *Look out for local or national resources which might help to make the activities more relevant to your particular group.*

6. If you are planning to organise remembrance events, public actions, or campaigns to address current injustices against the Roma, remember that such efforts will be strengthened by involving representatives from both the Roma and non-Roma communities. You could also try to link up with other youth groups or make contact with national or international NGOs working for Roma rights.

» Look out for potential partners, supporters, speakers or activists. Encourage participants to reach out to other groups or communities.

> Use the country data on page 109 to plan your own remembrance events, or to lobby for recognition of the Genocide by particular governments. More detailed information on local events can be found in the full CAHROM document available at http://hub.coe.int/web/coe-portal/cahrom1

7. You will be more likely to arouse participants' interest and help them to find ways of addressing the difficulties facing Roma today if you involve them in decisions about the learning process.

   » Be guided by the needs, interests, concerns and wishes of your group. Consult them regularly and find out how they would like to proceed.

8. Remember the sensitive nature of the topic and be alert to the possibility of participants being confused or upset. It is important to provide space within sessions to address any emotional concerns and to build a culture of support within the group. Let them know that you are available if necessary.

   » Do not forget the emotional aspects of the learning process, and make sure you address any emotions triggered by the process itself.

9. Despite continuing prejudice towards the Roma, and despite low levels of awareness of the Genocide, remember that there has in fact been progress in securing public recognition. This has largely come about as a result of pressure from the Roma community, including some notable efforts by committed individuals.

   » Mix the 'negative' messages of the Genocide itself with positive stories about those who have managed to bring it to public attention, and who have secured some compensation and acknowledgement.

10. Finally, any learning process is enhanced by encouraging participants to build on it afterwards. In the case of this topic, it is not only your participants that need to 'learn', it is society as a whole. Participants can contribute to that process, and will be greatly empowered by doing so.

    » Encourage participants to take the learning "out of the group". Help them to pass their own learning on to others.

> On 17 November, the Czech state holiday celebrating democracy and freedom, the Slave of Race (Otrokem Rasy) initiative participated in an event in Prague called the Velvet Fair. Our topic was the Romani Holocaust at Lety and our contribution was called 'SOMETHING STINKS HERE.'
>
> Slave of Race worked with a sculptor who designed a large pig whose nose was sealed shut with a clothespin, and masks depicting deceased Romani people. Our crew was led by figures dressed in black wearing white masks with question marks on them. They were pushing a carriage carrying a sound system broadcasting a political speech accompanied by the sound of pigs grunting and squealing.
>
> The song 'Ajgele Roma', which talks about Romani people traveling the world in search of cheer and happiness, rose like hope above these depictions of suffering.
>
> One viewer of the procession remarked, 'It was a very provocative spectacle which clearly showed that something is not right here. It reflected the burden of injustice, the absurdity of the existence of a pig farm on a place where such murder was committed, and also an admirable sense of the joy of life, which Romani people have preserved despite centuries of oppression'.
>
> *From RomaReact*

5.2 Planning your activities

There are numerous ways to work on the Roma Genocide. Almost all will be important and will make a useful contribution to this much neglected issue. However, different groups in different contexts will have different needs and interests and you may have specific outcomes that you also wish to be addressed, such as identity-related issues among Roma participants, a better awareness of the local history, or discrimination in society today.

Spend a little time considering the following:

What is the national or local context?	*For example*: how did the Genocide affect the Roma in your country? Has it been acknowledged by the Government? How are Roma communities treated today?
Are there useful resources which could support your work?	*For example*: is there a memorial site or former place of detention in the locality? Are there any local or national organisations which could speak to the group? Can you make contact with Roma communities or survivors of the Genocide?

What are the 'key messages' or key areas of understanding that you would like the activities to support?	*For example*: the role of individual actors during the Genocide, the link with discrimination against the Roma today, the importance of disseminating the message to the wider public, and so on.
How much time are you able to devote to the topic?	Make sure that you prioritise 'key messages' according to the time you have available. Do not try to achieve everything in just one session!

And perhaps above all …

What are the main interests or priorities for your group?	These questions are explored more fully in the next section.

5.3 Starting from where the group is

The aims and objectives for your activities will depend to a large extent on the nature of your group. If you have time available, consulting the group on their interests and finding out what they already know can be the most effective way to shape the learning process. If you have only one session, and the group is unfamiliar to you, a short brainstorming activity at the start will help you to obtain a clearer picture, and will also help participants to feel involved.

> The Ruhama Foundation supported over 76 Roma and non-Roma young activists from Romania in taking part in the Roma Genocide Remembrance Event "Dik I Na Bistar" ("Look and Don't Forget") which was held in Kraków in August 2013. As a result of the visit, participants were motivated to produce their own magazine about the Genocide. Thirteen young people wrote an article about their feelings, explaining what they thought needed to be done so that others "look and don't forget".

Try, at least, to take the following into account before planning the session:

- Are the participants Roma, non-Roma or mixed? How well do they inter-relate as a group?

- What are they likely to know already about the Roma Genocide?

- Do you know what their existing sympathies or prejudices are likely to be (towards the Roma, in particular)?

- What types of activity or what information are they likely to be engaged by and respond to best?

Roma and non-Roma groups

The issue of whether your group includes Roma participants, or is exclusively Roma, is an important one. There are benefits to working with Roma and non-Roma audiences separately, and benefits to working with mixed groups. However, given the nature of the topic, it is useful to be aware of the specific needs and likely pre-conceptions which participants might hold because of the way they self-identify. The following considerations may also be relevant to other ethnic groups, and in particular, to other groups that suffered in the Holocaust.

Make sure that you are sensitive to each of the following possibilities:

1. Non-Roma participants may have strong prejudices about the Roma.

If you are working with an exclusively non-Roma group, it may be necessary to address these prejudices directly even before providing information about the Holocaust. Sadly, a common response today to the difficulties and human rights violations experienced by Roma groups throughout Europe is that "they deserve it". This is of course the very reason why education in this area is so important.

> *Michelle Kelso describes the response of a group of Romanian educators to the screening of a film about the Genocide of the Romanian Roma:*
>
> "We hadn't expected overt discrimination to almost halt the screening before it even started, and to permeate almost all of the follow-up discussion after the film ... .
>
> The very roots of prejudice and discrimination that led to the Holocaust were still present in Romania. The discrimination that many Roma faced was distortedly viewed as "normal" by non-Roma."
>
> *Kelso, Michelle, L., "Recognizing the Roma: a study of the Holocaust as viewed in Romania", 2010*

With a mixed group, where prejudices are likely to exist, they will also need to be addressed. This is important not only because strong prejudice among some participants will affect how they perceive the message, but also because good relations between members of the group are essential in addressing topics of this sensitivity. A lack of trust, tact, sensitivity or solidarity on the part of any member of the group will make the task more difficult, and could even be counter-productive for the end result. Roma participants need to be able to feel that they can speak freely and that they are respected by others; non-Roma need to be open to the possibilities of fellow members of the group being hurt by certain expressions or attitudes.

- If you have more than one session available and are working with a group including non-Roma who are likely to have strong prejudices, consider starting with the activity on discrimination on page 88.

- If you are concerned that trust between participants is completely absent, consider running different sessions or talking separately with Roma and non-Roma participants before bringing them together.

2. Roma participants may be strongly affected by the information presented

If you have Roma participants in your group, you will need to be prepared to offer support in case any are upset by the information provided. This is particularly important if you are organising visits to sites where mass suffering or killing took place. In a mixed group, you should also alert non-Roma participants to the need to offer understanding and support.

- Activity 1 on page 74 offers a template for debriefing a visit to a memorial site or for debriefing another activity which has affected participants emotionally.

- Suggestions for preparing Holocaust Memorial Days can be found in a publication produced by ODIHR-OSCE, available at http://www.osce.org/odihr/44474

- Guidelines for teachers and educators are also collected in the Council of Europe publication, *European pack for visiting Auschwitz-Birkenau Memorial and Museum* www.coe.int/t/dg4/education/remembrance/archives/Source/Publications_pdf/European_Pack_en.pdf

---

Sefedin Jonuz describes a visit to Buchenwald with a group of Roma

"The first picture we saw showed a German fascist who was taking the eyes out of the head of a Romani woman and man. A small child stood next to them and had to watch this disgusting act. A woman fascist stood next to this child. As I read the caption of this picture, I was so shocked that I couldn't say a word and my tears began to flow and all the Roma, the whole group, gathered around me and asked what I saw in the picture and what was wrong with me. When I told them what was written there, they all cried deep from the soul, quietly, and they could only see their own tears."

Sefedin Jonuz, "Memory needs a place"

---

3. There may be different objectives for Roma and non-Roma participants

Most of the activities included in Chapter 6 are written with non-Roma groups, or mixed groups, as their primary audience. If you are working with Roma groups, it may be worth altering the emphasis in some of the activities to reinforce some of the messages in the following table:

Key messages for Roma participants
1. The Holocaust was something done *to* the Roma
It is very natural for sensitive human beings to be concerned that they may have been responsible for tragedies that have befallen them. You should emphasise that no-one who has been treated as the Roma were during the Holocaust should ever feel responsible for what happened, nor should anyone suggest that some of the behaviour was justified.
2. Roma participants should take pride in their identity
You could explore this further by asking participants to think about those aspects of their identity or ethnic group which appeal to them. Remind them, if necessary, that no-one is ever content with *all* the aspects of a group they self-identify with! You could also look at positive role models. (Use the information on the Rose Family on pages 34 - 35 or the links provided at the end of Activity 5 on page 80.)
3. Roma people can contribute to reshaping society
It is important that participants feel there are positive actions that they can take to affect their own lives, and to alter general attitudes towards the Roma. Alerting the public to the crimes of the Holocaust is one way of doing this; appealing to human rights standards is another.

5.4 Encouraging action

If educational work in this area is "successful", it will almost certainly trigger participants' interest and concern, and they are likely to want to explore the issue further and even to organise their own remembrance events or activities.

> On 1-4 August 2013, the international youth organisation TernYpe brought 430 participants from all over Europe to Kraków for several days of reflection and learning on the Roma Genocide. The event included workshops, lectures from expert speakers, a public conference and a visit to Auschwitz, culminating in a youth commemoration ceremony. Visit http://www.2august.eu/ for more information.
>
> *On the night of 2-3 August 1944, 2,897 Roma were murdered in the gas chambers of the 'Gypsy Camp' at Auschwitz-Birkenau.*

In many ways, this is the best overall aim for your work, and the best indicator that the work has been worthwhile. However, it is worth bearing in mind that a shortcut to action, in other words, concentrating exclusively on the action, may have less impact than a process which plants the desire in participants to do something themselves. As noted in Chapter 3, a purely 'symbolic' remembrance event is easy to organise; much harder is to initiate a process where your participants, and perhaps other members of the public, continue to 'remember' after the formal event has passed.

Some ideas for organising actions with the group can be found on pages 92 - 97, together with a template for a planning session.

5.5 Facilitation

Effective facilitation can make or break an educational process. In many ways, it is the single most important contribution you can make towards the way participants will understand and act upon the issues.

The following checklist is intended as a *reminder*. If you are unfamiliar with the idea of 'facilitation' or unaccustomed to a learning process which actively involves participants, refer to Chapter 1.4 of *Compass* for a more detailed explanation.

10 DOs and DON'Ts for effective facilitation:

Do encourage participants to voice their opinions and ideas.	Don't condemn any suggestions as "useless", "irrelevant" or "stupid"!
Do try to develop a culture of mutual respect, a safe environment where everyone feels comfortable about expressing their opinion.	Don't allow the group to exclude, ignore, prejudge, or disrespect anyone else: try to establish some basic principles from the outset.
Do encourage discussion and questioning: they will learn by expressing their doubts or uncertainty.	Don't try to give lengthy presentations: that will only turn them off!
Do make links with the reality of the participants and with real issues in their environment.	Don't hand out generalisations which they can't relate to.
Do abandon dogma! Allow them to question 'established truths', and do so yourself.	Don't "preach", or use your position to close an argument!

Do be honest with participants. They will respect you more and will be more likely to open up themselves.	Don't pretend to know if you aren't sure! Tell them you will find out, or encourage them to do so.
Do trust participants. They need to find the answers for themselves.	Don't talk down to them, and don't try to lead them where they won't be led.
Do take their suggestions seriously: they will be more likely to become involved if they feel ownership.	Don't feel you need to stick rigidly to what was planned: follow their interests if they prefer to move in another direction.
Do appeal to their natural human sympathies. Ask them how they feel, or how they *would* feel if … .	Don't give up if their opinions seem unkind or thoughtless; show them another perspective.
Do treat participants as equals – equal to each other, and 'equal' to you. You are all only human!	Don't exclude participants or make assumptions about what they can or can't do. Humans can be unpredictable!

6 Educational Activities

The activities in the next section have been divided into five key areas:

- **What happened?**
- **Why did it happen?**
- **Why was it wrong?**
- **How does it relate to today?**
- **What can we do?**

Each topic contains a series of questions which could be explored during the sessions or as part of a research project, and a few sample activities. Where time allows, you may want to combine different components of activities listed under separate sections.

Many activities will contain an element relating to each question area and all activities will be strengthened by including some discussion of the last two questions.

6.1 What happened?

Providing information on the Roma Genocide

It is likely that groups you work with will have little awareness of how the Roma were targeted and how they suffered. Information alone, without reflection, is unlikely to convey the full extent of the crimes committed, particularly if your group has its own prejudices about the Roma. Nevertheless, most activities will need to contain some informational aspect, and participants will certainly need to finish the session with a greater understanding of what actually happened. The diagram on page 72 outlines some of the more important issues which could be used as a focus for activities: do not attempt to address all of them in a single session!

How to 'present' information

In general, participants are more likely to have their interest aroused and retain the information if they have experienced or "worked with" it in some way, rather than simply having it presented by the facilitator. See below for some examples of "working with" information.

Participants carry out their own research	For participants unaccustomed to doing this, you can provide some useful websites and guiding questions for areas which they need to investigate. Small groups of participants could be given different areas to look at so that the group as a whole gains a fuller picture.
Using multimedia or non-textual sources	Drawing out information from images, videos or music can be more engaging than 'dry' texts, and these often convey a stronger emotional message. Ask participants to analyse information in different forms, extracting the most important facts. Use this to raise questions about interpretation, communication and subjectivity.
Using personal testimonies – either written or oral	If you have the possibility to organise discussions with those who themselves survived the Holocaust, or who have learned about it from survivors, this can be a powerful way of sending a personal message to participants. Ask them to draw up their own questions and guide them through the important points about conducting an interview. • If your group is Roma, invite them to talk to members of their own family or community to find out what they know. • Use some of the testimonies included in the Appendix at the end of this handbook.
Presenting information to others in the group – or to members of the public	Teaching others is one of the most effective ways of ensuring information is retained and understood. • Turn your participants into 'teachers' and ask them to convey the results of research they have carried out to others in the group, or to people outside the group. • Organising a public event or communicating with politicians, the media or local representatives can also be a useful way for participants to consider the important messages they would like to convey to others.

'Re-packaging' information in a different form	Presenting information does not need to be dull – either for those who are presenting or for those 'receiving'. • A personal testimonial can be turned into a drama project and the results of online research can be presented as a poem, song, image or collage. • The process can also go the other way: try giving participants several personal testimonials or images and ask them to imagine they are journalists and need to write an article telling the public about what is happening; or that they are human rights activists and need to write a report for a human rights committee.
Changing perspective	"Dry" historical facts can be made more relevant for participants by asking them to place themselves in the position of a Roma living at the time. A piece of text describing general conditions or forms of abuse can be used as the basis for creative writing, drama or other means of artistic expression. Ask participants to imagine this happened to them: *How would they feel? How would they behave? What would they want to say to the world?*
Organising outside visits	If there is a Holocaust-related site in your neighbourhood, or if you have the possibility to organise travel to others further away, such direct experience can be of great value. Some examples might include memorials, former concentration camps or places of deportation; remember, however, that even a walk around a neighbourhood which was affected by the Genocide can be a source of useful information.

6 Educational Activities

⚙ A1 — *These references relate to outline activities which can be used to explore some of the questions. A1 refers to Activity 1, A2 to Activity 2, etc.*

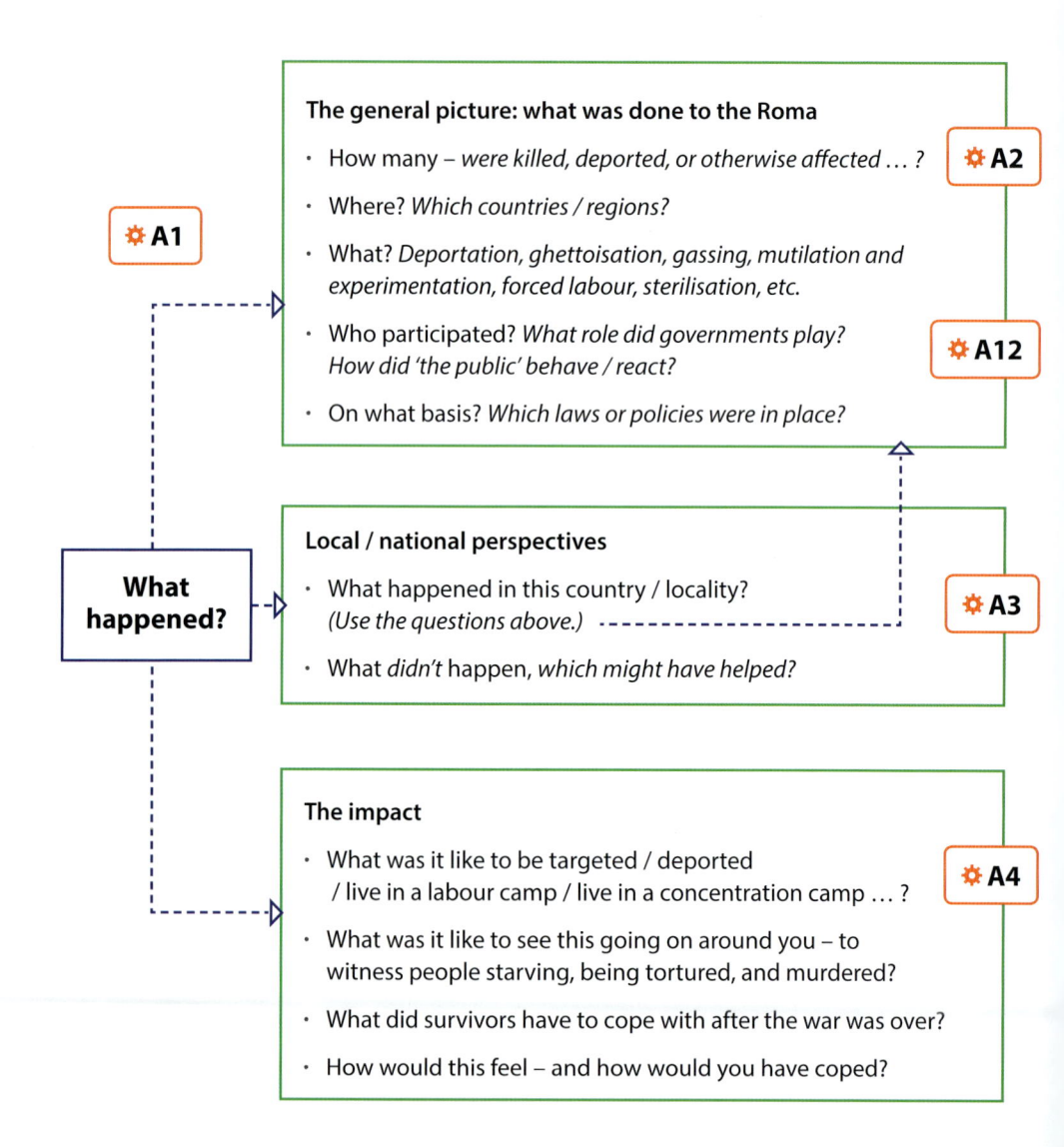

What happened?

⚙ A1 → The general picture: what was done to the Roma

- How many – *were killed, deported, or otherwise affected … ?* **⚙ A2**
- Where? *Which countries / regions?*
- What? *Deportation, ghettoisation, gassing, mutilation and experimentation, forced labour, sterilisation, etc.*
- Who participated? *What role did governments play? How did 'the public' behave / react?* **⚙ A12**
- On what basis? *Which laws or policies were in place?*

Local / national perspectives

- What happened in this country / locality? *(Use the questions above.)* **⚙ A3**
- What *didn't* happen, *which might have helped?*

The impact

- What was it like to be targeted / deported / live in a labour camp / live in a concentration camp … ? **⚙ A4**
- What was it like to see this going on around you – to witness people starving, being tortured, and murdered?
- What did survivors have to cope with after the war was over?
- How would this feel – and how would you have coped?

Suggestions for activities on 'what happened'

> From survivors we can get the real stories, which are connecting and linking us to lots of other related issues and discussions … . You see a story, you feel you are there, you are feeling the same, you just let people talk, as people have lots to say. These stories bring again the need to raise awareness of Roma youth to get them interested and motivated into the activities.
>
> *Dzafer Buzoli, from the organisation Youth for Positive Change*

The following brief activities can be used as starters for longer sessions, or can be expanded by you to explore issues in more detail.

The first activity outlines a debriefing session. This will be particularly useful after a visit to a Holocaust-related site but can also be adapted for use after any sessions which may have a strong emotional effect on participants.

A1 Activity 1: Debriefing session
For use after visits to Holocaust-related sites

- Try to run the debriefing session soon after the actual visit and make sure you have at least 30 minutes available. If possible, allow more time.
- Arrange the chairs in a circle so that participants can see each other and feel comfortable about speaking out. If participants do not know each other, ask them to introduce themselves briefly.
- Begin the discussion by recognising that participants may have experienced strong emotions during or after the visit. Reassure them that this is entirely natural. Explain that the session is intended to help participants to express and share feelings about the event, and to offer support, if necessary.
- Encourage everyone to share their feelings, but emphasise that no-one should feel obliged to do so. Tell them that nothing shared in the session will be taken out of the group – and ask everyone to respect this.
- Remind them that some participants may find it difficult to describe their emotions or may experience confusion in doing so. Ask for suggestions from the group about how the discussion can be most effective and about the kind of behaviour they expect from others. Try to agree on some basic 'rules' or principles for the discussion.
- Begin the discussion by asking if anyone would like to share their feelings, and offer the opportunity to anyone who wants to do so. Use some of the following questions, as appropriate, to continue the discussion, but do not be restricted by them! The most useful questions are likely to build on participants' responses.

  » What was most shocking or striking about the visit?
  » Did you see anything which was positive or encouraging?
  » What were your feelings at the time, and are they different now?
  » Do you think it was important to see this [site / memorial / survivor]? Why?
  » What do you feel you have taken away from the experience? Has it affected the way you look at anything else in your life?
  » Can you suggest anything you can do to act on the lessons you took away, or to disseminate this learning? Is this important to you?
  » Can you suggest anything that we can do as a group to follow up on this visit?

Remember to ensure …

  » That the discussion is not dominated by a few individuals and that you provide the opportunity for less confident participants to engage – perhaps by encouraging them directly.
  » To be sensitive to what is being said, why it is being said, and how it might affect others in the group. Offer your own comments where these seem to be necessary.
  » To let participants know that you are available if anyone wants to speak about their feelings more privately after the session.

Activity 2: The general picture
Using statistics to illustrate the impact and extent of the Genocide

- Ask participants to use the Internet to see if they can come up with approximate numbers for any of the following:
    - » Roma living in Europe before the Holocaust
    - » Roma deported / removed from their homes
    - » Roma murdered in the gas chambers
    - » Roma who died through other causes – for example starvation, disease, etc.
    - » Roma placed in labour camps or in segregated communities.
- If your country was one of those where Roma were targeted under the Genocide, participants could try to find figures for Europe as a whole and for your country.
- Tell them to record 'upper' and 'lower' estimates for each of the categories above.
- Show them the table on page 28; then use some of the following questions to discuss the information:
    - » Did you find it difficult to find statistics? What do you think is the reason for this?
    - » How do you explain the different estimates for Roma victims?
    - » What proportion of the Roma population were killed or otherwise affected by the Holocaust?
    - » If this group represents the Roma population before the Holocaust, how many of us would have been affected?
    - » How do you think others who survived the Holocaust would have felt?
    - » Which other groups or communities were targeted or murdered by the Nazis and their collaborators?
- You could mention the fact that statistics about Roma victims are very imprecise because of the way many of them died – and the absence of records. (See Section 2.2 for information)

A3 Activity 3: Local / national perspective
What happened here?

- If the Roma were targeted in your country during the Holocaust, ask them to explore what happened, for example:
  - Which forms and methods were used against the Roma? (e.g. deportation, mass murder, labour camps, etc. See pages 17 - 38 for information)
  - What did your government do and say at the time? What do they say about it now?
  - How did the public react?
  - Who stood up in defence of the Roma?
  - How many Roma were affected? How?
  - Did anything happen in your locality?
- If there were no obvious actions against the Roma in your country, participants could explore:
  - Whether your government commented at the time on the Roma Genocide, or took any action
  - What was said then – and now – about the Jewish and Roma victims. Has either group been supported and how, if at all, are these groups addressed in public speech and educational programmes?
  - What does the public know about the Roma experience during the Holocaust?
  - How are the Roma viewed and treated generally in your country today?

A youth group working with the *Institut für Sozialarbeit* carried out a research project on Helen Weiss, a Roma girl who was deported to 'Zigeunerlager Lackenbach' when she was 13 years old. They found her name in various registers but also identified missing files, where no records were available. The group visited Helen's foster parents' grave and the place where she was deported. Then they organised a public presentation of their findings and told the story of Helen in the form of a rap.

A4 Activity 2: The impact
Using testimonies to illustrate the personal experience

- Use Anuta Branzan's testimony on page 105 (or another). Give a brief introduction, if necessary, to explain that tens of thousands of Roma were deported to camps in occupied Soviet territories during the Second World War. The testimony describes a typical experience.
- Read it out to participants and ask for reactions:
    » What are your feelings about the experience described?
    » What words would you use to describe this kind of treatment?
    » What do you think someone who had lived through this as a child would feel afterwards about the society that did this to her?
    » What messages might she pass on to her children?
- Ask whether participants were aware that the Roma were targeted by the Nazi regime for complete 'elimination' – just as the Jews were. Give them some information about other forms of treatment they had to suffer, including being murdered in the gas chambers. Remind them that millions of Roma throughout Europe have to live with the memory of this brutal behaviour towards their people.
    » Ask whether participants could trust or 'forgive' a society which had behaved in such a way towards their own people.
    » Ask what might help someone to regain that trust, and come to terms with the experience: what would *you* want from society if it had happened to you?
- Invite participants to look into the ways that the Holocaust is remembered in their society – including memorials, remembrance days, educational resources, etc.
    » To what extent are the Roma victims remembered in any of these events or resources?
    » What message does this send to Roma people today, and what does it tell us about society?
- Participants could then think about how they could influence the way the Holocaust is remembered in their country. See Activity 12 for suggestions.

6.2 Why did it happen?

Understanding the causes

Understanding how such terrible events were able to occur also requires some awareness of historical detail. For example, of the way that laws and policies increasingly violated the rights of Roma communities from the 1920s onwards (and even before this). However, participants also need to be able to see the complexity of the processes and behaviours; to gain an understanding of the way the whole "machinery" operated and the dependence of this "machinery" on individual attitudes and forms of behaviour. This is particularly important because some of these attitudes, at least, are still present today in every country of Europe. The period leading up to the Holocaust was a time, after all, when general public attitudes towards the Roma were not dissimilar to those we find today. This question is explored further in the sections addressing the human rights connections with past and present (page 52).

> The sad truth is that most evil is done by people who never make up their minds to be good or evil.
>
> *Hannah Arendt, The Life of the Mind*

It is common to "explain" the Holocaust as the result of evil behaviour by a group of evil people. Although some of those who participated were certainly able to act in ways that no "normal" human being would countenance – the work of Dr Mengele stands out – participants need to see that single individuals could not have carried out these actions without at least the passive consent of hundreds of thousands, perhaps millions of others. It is both unlikely to be the case, and unhelpful for a deeper understanding to explain away this behaviour by branding all those who played a role as "evil".

How did it happen?

Structural factors

- What were the formal policies in place (in particular countries)?
- What was the official basis for the discrimination? *'Genetic' grounds, 'criminality', 'spies', etc.*
- How were people identified, collected, removed, controlled, murdered?
- How were the Roma treated before the Holocaust? *Poor living conditions for Roma, exclusion from many public services, discriminatory laws and negative public attitudes throughout Europe, etc.*
- How did this affect what happened during the Holocaust?

✱ **A12**

Psychological and behavioural factors

- How did members of the public react – or not react? *Why?* ✱ **A5**
- Who contributed to the "killing machine"? Was this a small sector of society / a group of "evil" people?
- What role did fear / punishment play? *Positive examples: occasional "heroes" who helped Roma victims – and were themselves punished.*
- What was the general public attitude towards the Roma ("gypsies")? *Would different attitudes have led to different results?* ✱ **A6**

Activities on the causes

⚙ A5 Activity 5: Behaviours
Who contributed?

- Remind participants that some people did offer support to Roma victims during the Holocaust. Although a few may have been punished for doing so, the fear of being punished was perhaps a bigger obstacle.
- Give participants a copy of the Handout at the end of this activity. Ask them to name a few of the non-Roma people "mentioned" in this passage who knew about what was happening and did nothing. You could also draw attention to the few train passengers who threw packages of food into the camp.
- Gather two or three examples then ask participants to work in small groups to expand the list, using ideas from the passage or other knowledge they may have about what happened. They should think about people who would need to have "known".
- Results could be presented in the form of a 'map' of the community: a large image of the different observers, indicating how they came to know.
- Encourage participants to think widely, imagining that such a terrible thing was happening today, and how *they* might come to hear about it. Their lists might include some of the following:
    - » Journalists on the newspapers
    - » All their readers
    - » Psychologists who undertook the research, and those others who must have read it
    - » Eye-witnesses to the visits by psychologists – including neighbours
    - » The train drivers
    - » All the passengers who did not throw food to camp inmates
    - » Guards at the camp – and other camp personnel
    - » Those who arrested the inmates and accompanied them to the camp
    - » Those who witnessed the arrests or the journey
    - » Those who saw the empty houses of Roma, or who noticed their absence
    - » The families and friends of anyone listed above
    - » … and so on.
- Ask participants to reflect on what would have happened if *all* of the above had refused to take part in the programme, or had objected to what was being done.
    - » How do you think you might behave if something like this ever happened again – and you knew about it?
    - » At what point would you intervene or raise your voice?
- Read out the second or third Handout about "supporters" or refer to the information from page 31 onwards to show participants that there some who did put themselves out to help the victims of the Holocaust. Ask for their comments.
- You could close by alerting participants to the fact that the gas chambers did not appear out of nowhere: there were indications for many years that the Roma were being subjected to severe discrimination and abuse. Do they see any parallels with today?

Handout for participants

"Whatever the real state of knowledge or ignorance among the German civilian population during the Second World War about the transport and the murder of millions of German and non-German Jews in Europe, the initial internment of the Roma was kept secret from no-one. Concentration camps were built on the outskirts of the capital city, and the internment of the Sinti and Roma was not only covered by a number of Berlin newspapers, but was even joked about in their columns. Psychologists engaged in racial research paid official visits to Marzahn to study and take extensive film footage of the Romani children at play there. A major trainline ran right past that camp, and its few survivors recall that train passengers who pitied their situation, and who knew or suspected that the interned Roma were surviving on only minimal rations, occasionally threw packages of food down into the camp enclosure as their train passed by."

Katie Trumpener, The time of the Gypsies: "A People without History" in the narratives of the West

A Police Officer

"With the help of friends and neighbours, some Sinti and Roma managed to go underground to escape impending deportation. They were sometimes warned by officials who deliberately delayed or circumvented the execution of the deportation orders. Paul Kreber, who worked for the police in Wuppertal, was one of them. He refused to carry out deportation orders and helped the persecuted to flee."

http://www.sintiundroma.de

A Camp Official

"The last *Lagerfuhrer* ... in the Gypsy camp [at Auschwitz] was Bonigut .... He did not agree with the SS tactics. He was a very good man. On May 15, 1944, he came up to me and told me that the situation in the Gypsy camp was bad. The decision to liquidate the Gypsy camp had been made .... The camp then numbered about 6,500 Gypsies. Bonigut recommended that I inform absolutely trustworthy Gypsies about this. He recommended that I warn them 'not to go like lambs to the slaughter' ... .

The next day, the *Lagerfuhrer* came up to me and ... ordered me to draw up a list of Gypsies who had served in the German army and been decorated. The list also included the families of those Gypsies, as well as the families of those who were still on active service ... . The list contained the names of about 3,200 men, women and children. A few days later, a commission made up of SS men from the political department came to the Gypsy camp. The commission also included Dr Mengele. All the Gypsies on the list were summoned to the entrance gate. They were allowed to take all their belongings, such as clothing, pots and pans, and so on."

Tadeusz Joachimowski, Polish former prisoner and clerk at the Zigeunerlager

Activity 6: The role of public attitudes

What's in a name?

- Read out the narrative on page 44. Ask participants whether the example seems absurd: would anyone ever be treated in this way just because of their name!?
- Explain that although the narrative is semi-fictional, the experience it describes is one that has been shared by thousands of people, some of whom are still alive today. Tell them – if they have not guessed – that the description is a typical example of what Roma survivors of the Holocaust might have been through.
- Ask for reactions and explore whether the analogy of a family name is relevant:
    » Would the treatment be more "reasonable" if the 'name' referred to an ethnic identity rather than membership of a particular family?
    » Why should we feel it is absurd to condemn someone for their surname, but reasonable to do so for their ethnic identity?
    » What do you think about people in other countries who refer to people from *your* country as … [*insert the most common negative stereotype about participants' nationality here*].
- Tell participants that scientists have found no evidence that people can be divided according to 'race' and that the term is now understood to be a social construct. Still, some people think they can predict what someone will be like just because of what they look like, or which group they affiliate with.
- You could provide some information on the genetic theories developed by the Nazis and about Dr Mengele's experimentation on Roma children. Use the testimony on page 26 to convey the barbaric nature of these crimes.
- Ask what the activity has told participants about the dangers of labelling people, or making assumptions when we have no evidence to back it up.
    » Do you think "labelling" of Roma still takes place in your country?
    » How much do people really know about the Roma, and how much do *you* know?
    » How can we encourage people to stop thinking in terms of labels, and to look at people as they really are? How would *you* go about this?
- Use the discussion as a lead-in to one of the following themes:
    » Human rights: explaining the core value of equality (or non-discrimination)
    » Roma identity: you could suggest that participants try to find out more about the Roma, exploring some of the positive aspects. Invite someone from a Roma community to speak to the group if this is possible, or use the links below to look at positive role models. Ask what such individuals tell us about the dangers of making generalisations about "all Roma". http://www.imninalu.net/famousGypsies.htm or http://romove.radio.cz/en/article/18243
    » The history of the Roma Genocide: exploring how attitudes such as those already discussed contributed to what happened.

6.3 Why was it wrong?
Human rights and the moral aspect

It is important that both Roma and non-Roma participants understand that what happened during the Holocaust was deeply wrong, and that there can be no justification or excuse. This is obviously an important message for non-Roma – not least because without that understanding, the discrimination and abuse experienced by the Roma today cannot be addressed.

However, the human rights message is also important for Roma participants because victimisation can sometimes lead to self-blaming. It is vital to convey the message that the way the Roma population was treated was an abuse of every moral standard – and that this has since been recognised by societies around the world (in words, if not in deeds).

Human rights can help to confirm this message – for participants from any community. They provide a benchmark for acceptable behaviour which has been endorsed by every government in the world. Reminding participants that the fact that this consensus exists – and that it arose partly as a result of the crimes committed during the Holocaust – can send an important message.

If time allows, a whole session which looks at the values at the heart of human rights and the protections they offer will be useful. You can use the activities suggested in Activity 7 (below), or take a look at some of the resources listed in the Links section.

Why was it wrong?

Human rights — A7

- What do human rights say about the worst crimes committed against the Roma? *Absolute rights: the right to life and freedom from torture*
- What do they say about racism and discrimination? *The principle of equality, the role of stereotypes and prejudice*
- Which other rights were violated for Roma people during (and before) the Holocaust? *Non-discrimination, right to life, right to be free from torture and inhuman and degrading treatment, etc.*
- What do human rights demand from individuals?
- How can human rights help to prevent such things happening again? — A8

Moral principles

- Which moral principles would we like others to be guided by in their relations towards us? *Equality, respect, fairness, solidarity, etc.*
- How do these principles relate to human rights?
- Which of these principles were violated in the way the Roma were treated during the Holocaust? — A9
- Is the kind of treatment suffered by the Roma ever justified in moral terms or human rights terms?
- What is demanded from us if these principles are to be generally respected?

A7 Activity 7: Introducing Human Rights
Roma human rights

- If participants are unfamiliar with human rights, run an introductory activity to familiarise them with some of the key ideas. You could use one of the following:
    - 'Race for Rights' in *Bookmarks*, the Council of Europe manual on hate speech online
    - 'Act it Out' or 'Draw-the-word' from *Compass* (http://www.coe.int/compass)
    - 'Advertising human rights', 'Red Alert' or 'What If?' from *Compasito* (http://www.coe.int/compasito)

Follow-up

- As part of the same session, or as a research project, invite participants to explore organisations working to protect Roma human rights at local, national or international level. Ask them to record the following information:
    - Which level the organisation works at (and whether it covers their country)
    - Which issues / rights the organisation works on
    - The methods used by the organisation to carry out its work
    - Any notable successes.
- Alternatively, the research could be confined to organisations working on the Roma Genocide.
- Participants could also look at whether there are ways they can interact with any of these organisations. If any exist within your region, consider inviting someone to come and speak to the group.

Activity 8: Human rights and the Holocaust

Mapping the rights

- Ask participants to think about the different members of a family that they know well, which may be their own. Ask them whether they can find something common to *everyone* in this family.
- If there are any such characteristics, would it be right to conclude that *any* new child born into this family must also possess these characteristics?
- Ask them to consider what their reaction would be if someone met one of them for the first time, and said the following:

    "I know both your parents and I knew your grandparents. I taught all your cousins and your brothers and sisters. I know exactly what you must be like."

    » How would they feel?
    » Do they like to be "categorised" by others who do not know them properly?
    » Why does it feel wrong when people do this?

- Explain briefly the terms 'racism', 'stereotype' and 'discrimination' and ask if participants can think of common prejudices about the Roma which exist in society today.
- Ask what they would think about the following claim:

    "I have had Roma children in my class and I have seen them in the neighbourhood. I know exactly what they are all like."

    » How is this statement different from the one above about knowing you?

- Explain that after the Second World War, an international set of standards was established, agreed by all countries of the newly-formed United Nations. The standards are known as human rights and were supposed to ensure that nothing like the Holocaust ever happened again.
- Either as part of this activity or as a follow-up activity, give participants an abbreviated version of the UDHR (or the ECHR) and ask them to identify any rights which they believe were violated during the Roma Genocide. They all were, but you may want to ask participants to research further if they are unsure of specific examples to illustrate some of the violations. Some information is included on page 50 of this handbook.
- Pay particular attention to the Articles which forbid discrimination (Articles 1 and 2 in the UDHR, Article 14 and Protocol 12 in the ECHR).

A9 Activity 9: Moral principles
Unwrapping the crimes

- Ask participants to "unwrap" some of the crimes committed against the Roma (see page 52, 'Unwrapping the moral crimes' for an example). How many things that were "wrong" can they identify?
- Then ask them to think about what might be needed for victims of such crimes: what is the least that society could do to compensate each of them?
- Give the group some information about recognition of the Roma Genocide starting on page 109. Emphasise the important role that Roma organisations – and individuals – have played in achieving recognition of the Roma Genocide. Ask whether participants can think of things the group could do to support these efforts and bring the information to a wider public.

6.4 How does it relate to today?

Understanding the relevance

> These are dark-skinned people, not Europeans like you and me! Our final goal is to have zero Gypsy camps in Milan.
>
> *Riccardo De Corato, deputy vice mayor of Milan, Italy (October 2010)*

> Maybe Hitler didn't kill enough of them.
>
> *Gilles Bourdouleix, mayor of Cholet, France (July 2013)*

> If the Roma have no money on them when apprehended, they should be expelled immediately.
>
> *Lars Barfoed, former justice minister and deputy prime minister, Denmark (July 2010)*

> A significant part of the Roma are unfit for coexistence. They are not fit to live among people .... These animals shouldn't be allowed to exist. In any which way. That needs to be solved - immediately and regardless of the method.
>
> *Zsolt Bayer, co-founder of the Fidesz Party, Hungary (January 2013)*

Educating for remembrance is partly about giving young people an understanding of the terrible past events which continue to influence some people's lives today; and partly about helping them to identify patterns in their own behaviour which recall some of the underlying reasons for the Genocide. The section 'How should we remember' (page 46) outlines in detail how remembrance can contribute to this task, for the benefit of the Roma population and for others in society.

However, work on this theme can have an even wider impact if the members of your group also become 'ambassadors' for the topic, and feel the need to disseminate the message further. For this task, they will be helped by considering how their "messaging" will best address the negative attitudes or forms of behaviour which are most pressing for society.

The questions and activities in this section look both at the problem of discrimination against the Roma today, and at the "messages" which society needs in order to address existing prejudice. The aim is for participants to see the necessity of altering current injustices and patterns of discrimination against the Roma.

Why does it matter today?

Racism and discrimination today
- What are general attitudes towards Roma like today?
- What are the common forms of discrimination against the Roma – and in which countries of Europe do they occur?
- Why is this unacceptable?
- Are there any parallels with the Holocaust – or the years leading up to the Holocaust?
- What should be done to address racism and discrimination against the Roma today?
- What can *we* do and what should governments do?

A10

Acknowledgement and compensation
- Why is it important for people to know about the Roma Genocide?
- What are the key messages for society in 'remembering' the Holocaust?
- What are the key messages for the Roma community?
- What would 'compensation' involve, if it was to provide some remedy for the treatment suffered?
- What can individuals do?

A11

Activities on the relation to today

✦ A10 Activity 10: Antigypsyism today
Foreign Child

- Make copies of the Handout 'Foreign child' (below) and of the abbreviated version of the ECHR. Prepare a piece of flipchart paper for each small group and stick the information about 'Foreign child' in the middle of the flipchart paper.
- Read out the story to participants and ask them to guess the minority. Tell them that all the examples are typical of Roma experiences in countries throughout Europe (and the world).
- Ask for brief reactions to the text and explain that most of the examples are illegal under human rights law and illegal in every country in Europe.
- Ask participants to create small working groups – about 5 people in each group – and give each group one of the pieces of flipchart paper with the text about Group X. Ask them to mark on the flipchart paper, near the text, any connections between parts of the child's story and particular human rights.
- When groups have finished, stick up the finished flipchart papers on the wall and give participants the opportunity to look at those done by other groups, and to note any similarities or differences.
- Use some of the following questions to debrief the activity.

For non-Roma groups:

» Were you surprised by the number of different abuses which members of the Roma community commonly experience? Do you think any / all of these examples happen in this country?

» Imagine you heard or came across a nasty comment about "the Roma": what would you do? Do you think it would make a difference if people started objecting to such comments?

» Those who drew up the UDHR also thought that there were certain things we shouldn't do to anyone, however they may have behaved. Do you agree?

» How do you think you would feel if you were constantly abused by others in the community? How might you behave?

For Roma groups:

Use the narrative and the mapping activity to reassure participants that although this type of behaviour is still very common, there is at least "official" acknowledgement by governments around the world that it is unacceptable. There have also been many successes by organisations and individuals in working to combat racism and discrimination against the Roma.

Use some of the following questions to explore the issues:

» Have you ever experienced anything like that described in the story?

» Did you know that much of this behaviour is a human rights violation – and illegal?

» Does this make a difference to how you see the behaviour? Does it help that there is at least formal recognition that it is unacceptable?

» Do you have other examples not mentioned in the text of ways you have been treated unfairly? Do you think any of these were human rights violations?

- » Do you know of any organisations or individuals working to combat behaviour like this? Can you list any successes?
- » How can you make use of the information about human rights to support members of your community?
- Tell participants about some of the organisations working on Roma human rights, or ask them to carry out some research themselves. See Activity 7 for some guidelines.
- For both groups, use the resource sheet 'Rights Engaged' on page 90 to feed back on the prepared flipcharts. Note that many of the abuses in the story engage more than one right, and that nearly all of them engage the right to be free from discrimination.

HANDOUT: FOREIGN CHILD

I'm told I am a foreigner, although I was born here and so were my parents. At school, I've been put in a special class for "foreign" children – so have my brothers and sisters. We're not allowed to be in "normal" classes. We all get bullied by the other children because we're *different*. The teachers don't do anything about it. Some teachers even pick on us. *They* never get punished.

People don't want us around. They don't even know us, they just shout at us or beat us up because of who we are – or who they think we are. Well, we're children, just like them. And how are we meant to behave if someone shouts at us or beats us up? Should we like them for it?

If we go to the police, they often don't listen. They tell us it must have been our fault because we're all trouble makers. How do they know? I thought the courts were meant to decide that. The police stop us in the streets all the time for no reason. They tell us they think we've stolen something and they need to search us. Sometimes I get stopped six times a day but I've never stolen anything.

I've heard of people like me who've been in prison and have been beaten up by prison officers. Why should someone who beats up someone else not be punished? Even prison officers are meant to obey the law.

Members of the government often slag us off. As if everyone from my community is the same, everyone is a criminal. Well, we're not. *Every* community has some people who commit crimes. The government doesn't slag off "everyone" in another community, just because a few of them commit crimes. Why don't they ever tell the good stories? Or the normal stories? Our normal stories are good – just like theirs are.

On the television and on the Internet, people just say whatever they want about us. I'm sick of seeing Facebook groups telling us we're dirty or stupid or much worse things. They tell us we should get out of the country, go home, get a job like everyone else. My Dad would love to have a job. No-one will employ him because he's "foreign".

How are we supposed to live? How are we meant to feel when everyone says nasty things about us, even when they don't know us? It's hard: sometimes I don't want to go out into the street because I'm afraid I might get shouted at or beaten up.

'Solution' sheet: Rights Engaged

All examples are likely to engage the right to be free from discrimination (Article 13 or Protocol 12 of the European Convention of Human Rights). Other rights which may be engaged:

Special classes or schools for Roma children	Protocol 1, Article 2 (right to education)
Teachers picking on children	Article 8 (Private life). If the abuse is very bad, Article 3 (freedom from inhuman and degrading treatment). If it is affecting their education, may also engage Protocol 1, Article 2
Teachers not being "punished"	If no-one is taking complaints seriously, Article 8 (right to private life) or Article 3, if the abuse is very bad. Possibly Protocol 1, Article 2
People "shouting at" Roma	Article 8 if the abuse is bad, is happening regularly, and if the police is doing nothing about it
People beating them up	Article 8 if the police are not responding to complaints. If the beating up is very bad or happening regularly, Article 3
The police not listening to complaints	Article 8 or 3, depending on how bad the complaint is. If there are any threats to people's life, Article 2
The police stopping and searching Roma	Article 5 (Liberty) if people are being stopped very regularly for no good reason. Also Article 8
Prison officers beating up Roma	Article 3 if the beating up is very bad. Also Article 8
Prison officers not being "punished"	Article 3 if the beating up is very bad. Also Article 8
Members of the government abusing Roma	Article 8 if the abuse is very bad and is affecting how others treat Roma people
Abuse on the Internet / in the media	This may not be a strict violation of human rights because it is not a public official who is responsible. The abuse would have to be very bad, and there would need to be formal complaints which have been ignored by public officials
Not being able to get a job "because you're Roma"	Article 8 – particularly if any governmental organisations are refusing to employ someone because they are Roma
Being afraid to go out into the streets	If there is a real threat for Roma children on the streets and the police are doing nothing about it, this may engage Article 8 or 3 (or even 2 – right to life)

11 Activity 11: Acknowledgement

Messages to survivors

- Give participants a brief introduction to the Roma Genocide – if they are unaware of what happened. Explain that you will read them an account from someone who was a child at the time of the Holocaust. You could use one of those included in the Appendix or refer to the Links section.
- Read out the text, or give it to participants to read. Give them some quiet time to reflect on their own feelings after they have heard it.
- After a few minutes, ask if anyone would like to share their thoughts.
  - » What do they feel about what they have heard?
  - » Were they aware that Roma people were treated in this way?
  - » What do they think that someone who had experienced this might want to hear from society? Which messages might be helpful or supportive?
- Tell them that they are asked to compose a response to the author of the piece. This may take any form, for example, it could be a painting, a poem, or a letter. Tell them that this should be as personal as possible, and that no-one will have to share their work if they do not want to.
- Try to create a quiet space and encourage people to reflect and work on their own. If some are uneasy about this, allow them to work with others.
- If there is time available, you could allow participants to carry out some research into the context of the narrative: the countries where the events happened, or the camps themselves.
- At the end of the session, ask if anyone would like to share their work with the group.
- Close by asking if participants feel that the message they wanted to send is one that Roma people are receiving from society. Why, or why not? Can they do anything to influence the government or others in their community so that a different message goes out?

6.5 What can we do?

Encouraging participants to take action as part of, or as a result of the learning process will greatly increase the effectiveness of your work. 'Taking action' can mean anything that takes the learning outside the group and engages members of the public. It may include an awareness-raising event among a wider group, lobbying, petitioning or protesting, organising a demonstration or other public event, monitoring, reporting or submitting official complaints, or anything else designed to lead to some change in the outside world.

Taking action is an important part of remembrance education – and human rights education – partly because it increases the number of 'learners' and has the potential to alter society as a whole, even if only very slowly. Taking action, however, is also an important process for your group and can greatly help to consolidate any learning process. Participants will come to see the relevance of the issues discussed to life in the real world; they will reorganise and re-assess any understanding gained by thinking about the messages they want to convey to a wider public; they will gain new skills of effective communication and participation and they will come to perceive the importance of their own contribution. They may even manage to see the change they are helping to bring about and will be greatly empowered by the experience.

The next diagram indicates just some of the ways that young people can act on some of the issues relating to the Roma Genocide. There are many others!

6 Educational Activities

What can you do?

Raise awareness more widely – organise events such as:
- Remembrance events
- Exhibitions and readings
- Meetings and conferences
- Film showings / drama performances / concerts
- Silent vigils, reading of the dead
- Educational / awareness-raising activities

Lobbying public officials / campaigning on the Genocide:
- For remembrance education / dissemination of information about the Genocide
- For Roma Genocide Day to be officially marked
- For Holocaust memorials to record the Roma victims / for memorials to Roma victims
- For Holocaust Memorial Day to recognise the Roma suffering
- For the state to recognise its past role in the Genocide
- For journalists and public figures to speak out on the Genocide

Act against racism and discrimination today
- Speak out against racism, discrimination and hate speech
- Raise awareness of antigypsyism and campaign for equal rights
- Use art, drama, music, dance – or words – to spread positive messages about the Roma and Roma culture
- Report abuse to human rights organisations
- Join existing campaigns, such as the No Hate Speech Movement of the Council of Europe, or campaigns against evictions, racism, police brutality, etc.
- Monitor hate speech online – and report to Hate Speech Watch, http://www.nohatespeechmovement.org
- Call out politicians or public figures who make racist remarks
- Challenge journalists to report positively on the Roma
- Educate for Roma rights and human rights
- Publicise existing forms of discrimination, through leaflets, public events, online, etc.
- Make links with Roma groups and organise joint actions

Organising a remembrance event

> We have a 3x2 metre banner that reads 'Demolish the pig farm on the site of the Roma death camp in Lety!' and has a picture of Roma children murdered in Lety camp. We hang this banner during our meetings and events. We also used this banner during the Roma Pride Prague in 2012 and 2013.
>
> We also started a petition for demolishing the pig farm. We have been collecting signatures since October 2013.
>
> We visit Lety every year with young people from the communities. As a result of this, Lety has been written into a song by the De La Negra hip-hop crew – a group of young Konexe members, which has become quite famous in the Czech Roma Ghettos. (see http://youtu.be/x2EfDbANFls)
>
> *Konexe, a Roma youth organisation in the Czech Republic*

The final activity provides a generic form for planning an action related to the Roma Genocide. It can also be used to address the discrimination which Roma communities face today.

The activity is divided into 3 parts:

- Part 1: An introductory session, where participants look at issues or concerns that might form the focus of a public action. The activity proposed in Part 1 could also be replaced by others: the point is only to give participants a springboard for discussion, and some deeper understanding of an issue which they can use in planning the action.

- Part 2: Planning the action, where participants think through the aims and details of the action. Although many actions may be effective if they are spontaneous or undertaken with minimal planning, the planning process can be valuable both in increasing the effectiveness of the action, and in supporting young people to be more strategic in their aims.

- The structure of this part is based on Chapter 3 of *Compass* – Taking Action. You can use the guidelines under the section, 'Getting Results' for more detailed ideas. This is available at http://www.coe.int/compass.

- Part 3: A debriefing session after the event.
  It is very important to debrief any action once it has been carried out, and to debrief the process leading up to it. Many one-off actions can appear to have little effect and the group may become discouraged. You can use a debriefing session to address any concerns that participants may have that the action "was not worth doing" or that it "went badly". Remind them that campaigns typically consist of numerous actions and activities, all of which, when taken together, can help to change behaviours and attitudes.

12 Activity 12: Organise a remembrance event
Dosta!

Part 1: Preparation (optional: you could use another activity to introduce the action).

- Make copies of the Handout, 'Anti-Roma laws and policies in Germany' (pages 39 - 40).
- Ask participants to form small groups of 2 to 3 people who share the same sense of identity. This may relate to their ethnicity or nationality, or may be connected with different social or religious groupings (even football teams!). Ask them to share their feelings about this identity within their small groups.
- Give participants the Handout or present some of the information to give them a feeling for the successively brutal treatment that had to be endured by the Roma population. Do not tell them yet the name of the population that was targeted.
- Briefly discuss reactions. Then ask each group to pair up with another and discuss the following questions:
  » What would they feel if "their" people had been the target of this kind of treatment at some point in recent history? (Ask them to concentrate on the group they selected in the first group discussions.)
  » What do they feel would be the most difficult aspects for a community that had lived through this?
- Bring the group together and ask them to feed back on their discussions. Do they know, or can they guess which people the Handout referred to? If they do not guess, tell them it was the Roma, and ask what they know about the situation of Roma people today.
- Tell them that there have been cases in the European Court of Human Rights which have found numerous violations of human rights against the Roma in almost every country of Europe. Remind participants that the media and the population as a whole have very intolerant attitudes towards Roma people and they are frequent targets of abuse and hate crime. Ask if participants have come across any examples, in their media or in their own lives.
- Debrief this part of the activity by asking participants about their general reactions. Use some of the following questions:
  » Did the activity alter your attitudes towards Roma people?
  » Why do you think the suffering of the Roma people under the Nazi regime is so little known today?
  » Do you think if this was more widely known it would make a difference to the way Roma people are treated today?
  » What can you do to make the information more widely known?

Part 2: Planning a public action

- Make copies of the flowchart, or draw an empty version on a piece of flipchart paper.
- Explain that the group will be designing a public action to address one of the problems discussed in the first part of the activity.
- Ask them to brainstorm some of the issues which arose and which they would like to address. Explain that they will need to select one issue to work on.
- Discuss the most popular solutions briefly and try to reach consensus on one that all members will be happy to work with.
- Hand out copies of the flowchart on page 97, or use an empty version on a piece of flipchart paper. Use the headings in the flowchart and work through each box with participants. Check that:
    » The action they have identified will contribute to resolving the problem
    » The action is realistic, given the resources of the group and given the obstacles they may come up against
    » The 'solution' is concrete enough so that they will know whether they have achieved it or not.
- Draw up a Decision Sheet, so that everyone knows what they are supposed to be doing, and when. See the end of the Taking Action section of Compass for a model http://www.coe.int/compass.
- Debrief the planning session to check everyone is happy with the process and the result, and ready to implement the plan.

Part 3: Debriefing the action

- Begin the session by asking participants to describe their feelings after the day of action. This can be done briefly round the group, one by one.
- Divide participants into groups of 4-5 people and give them the following questions to discuss as a small group.
    » What did you feel went well?
    » Was there anything which was more difficult than you had imagined it to be, or anything unexpected?
    » What do you think were the main achievements of the action? Do these fit with the objectives you set out initially?
    » Do you think there are any lessons we could learn for next time?
- Bring the small groups back and discuss the different response to the questions. Finish the session with a few general impressions about the whole process:
    » Do you feel satisfied with your work in planning and carrying out this action?
    » What would you list as the main 'learning points' if you were to organise another action (on any theme)?
    » What have been the most important results for you personally? Do you feel that your views or attitudes have changed in any way?
    » How do you think it would be possible to build on what you have done? Do you feel interested to do this?

Planning your action

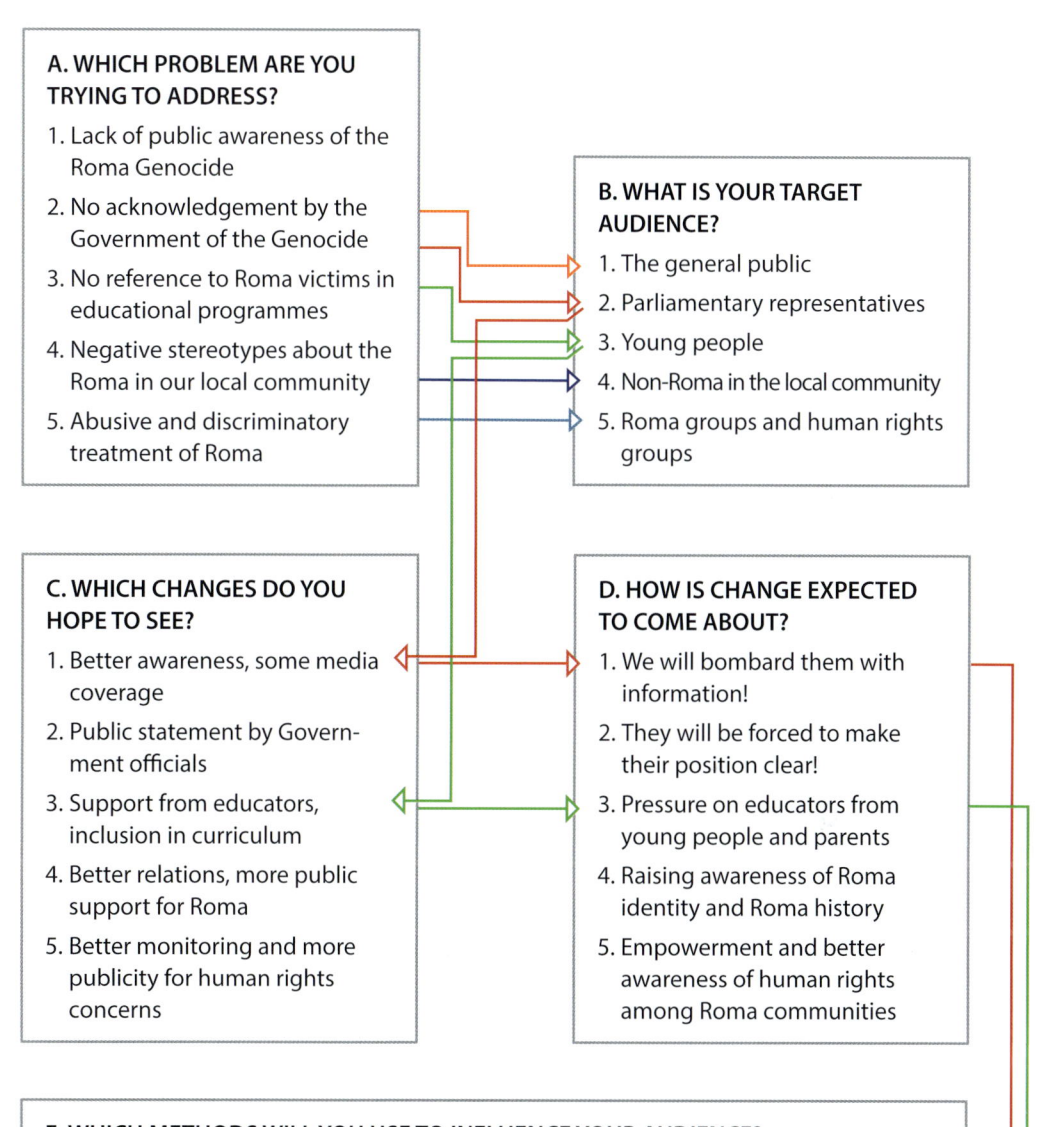

A. WHICH PROBLEM ARE YOU TRYING TO ADDRESS?

1. Lack of public awareness of the Roma Genocide
2. No acknowledgement by the Government of the Genocide
3. No reference to Roma victims in educational programmes
4. Negative stereotypes about the Roma in our local community
5. Abusive and discriminatory treatment of Roma

B. WHAT IS YOUR TARGET AUDIENCE?

1. The general public
2. Parliamentary representatives
3. Young people
4. Non-Roma in the local community
5. Roma groups and human rights groups

C. WHICH CHANGES DO YOU HOPE TO SEE?

1. Better awareness, some media coverage
2. Public statement by Government officials
3. Support from educators, inclusion in curriculum
4. Better relations, more public support for Roma
5. Better monitoring and more publicity for human rights concerns

D. HOW IS CHANGE EXPECTED TO COME ABOUT?

1. We will bombard them with information!
2. They will be forced to make their position clear!
3. Pressure on educators from young people and parents
4. Raising awareness of Roma identity and Roma history
5. Empowerment and better awareness of human rights among Roma communities

E. WHICH METHODS WILL YOU USE TO INFLUENCE YOUR AUDIENCE?

1. A high profile public event and targeting of the media
2. We will gather support from international organisations and members of the public
3. We will work with young people to raise questions at home and at school
4. An exhibition of Roma contributions in the local community – and a history of discrimination
5. Roma will be better informed about human rights and will make violations public

7 The Council of Europe, Education and Remembrance of the Roma Genocide

The Council of Europe and remembrance

The Council of Europe, which emerged from the ruins of the Second World War, has defined its fundamental objectives with a view to countering the totalitarian ideologies that dominated the first half of the 20th century and their corollaries: intolerance, separation, exclusion, hatred and discrimination, and mass human rights violations.

The values which the Council of Europe stands for – democracy, human rights and the rule of law – are part of preventive efforts to guarantee the construction of European societies striving to learn to respect the equal dignity of all.

The Council of Europe and remembrance of the Roma Genocide

Remembrance of the Roma Genocide connects with various areas of the work of the institution in the field of education and awareness-raising. Most can be grouped under education for democratic citizenship and human rights education. However, this wide approach sometimes hides the specific issues, approaches and contents related to the legacies of the racist past of Europe as found, for example, in anti-racist education, intercultural education and education about the Holocaust.

The Council of Europe carries out programmes of education and capacity building for various social actors, including educational professionals or youth organisations.

Training and supporting youth organisations and empowering young people to take action is an important part of the work done on this topic, especially through the activities of the two European Youth Centres and through the support offered by the European Youth Foundation. The aim of these activities supported by the Council of Europe is that young people can become aware of recent history and their role today for a culture of human rights. They can also take action for the recognition of the Roma and organise events for the commemoration days of the Roma Genocide.

The Council of Europe has also developed some relevant educational resources:

- The *Factsheets on Roma History*, a publication with an extensive history of the Romani people, with useful information regarding recent history and the Holocaust

- An online database of teaching materials on Roma history and culture, pedagogical materials and a virtual library. This project was developed jointly by the Council of Europe and OSCE - ODIHR.

- The Education Pack *All Different – All Equal* and *Compass*, two manuals on human rights education, include activities related to remembrance and combating discrimination through intercultural learning.

At political and policy levels

At political and policy levels, some examples of the work of the Council of Europe include:

- Recommendation Rec(2001)15 of the Committee of Ministers to member states on history teaching in twenty-first century Europe, which sets standards and guidelines for this type of education at a general level. The Committee of Ministers' Recommendation (2009)4 for member states promotes the inclusion of the Roma Genocide in Holocaust education and history teaching.

- Policy Recommendation no. 13 on combating antigypsyism and discrimination against Roma, by the European Commission against Racism and Intolerance, which states in its chapter on Curriculum, teaching material and teacher training that "Roma history and culture should be appropriately reflected in the general curriculum, including teaching about the Roma extermination as part of the Holocaust / Genocide of Roma".

The Council of Europe often also partners with other international institutions or networks, such as OSCE – Office for Democratic Institutions and Human Rights or the European Roma and Travellers Forum.

Appendix 1: Human Rights Documents

Universal Declaration of Human Rights (abbreviated version)

1. All human beings are born free and equal in dignity and rights.
2. Everyone has the right to be free from discrimination (fair and equal treatment). This includes discrimination on grounds of race, colour, sex, language, religion, political opinion, property, birth, or other status.
3. Everyone has the right to life and to live in freedom and safety.
4. No-one should treat anyone else as their slave
5. No-one should torture anyone else or treat them in an inhuman or degrading way.
6. Everyone has the right to recognition by the law.
7. The law is the same for everyone; it should be applied in the same way to all.
8. Everyone has the right to an effective remedy when his/her rights have not been respected.
9. No-one should be detained or imprisoned unjustly or expelled from their own country.
10. Everyone has the right to a fair and public trial.
11. Everyone should be considered innocent until found guilty.
12. Everyone has the right to have their privacy (including home and family life) respected.
13. Everyone has the right to live and travel freely within state borders.
14. Everyone has the right to go to another country and ask for protection if they are being persecuted or are in danger of being persecuted.
15. Everyone has the right to a nationality.
16. Everyone has the right to marry and have a family.
17. Everyone has the right to own property and possessions.
18. Everyone has the right to believe whatever they wish (including, but not confined to religion).
19. Everyone has the right to say what they think and to give and receive information freely.
20. Everyone has the right to join associations and to meet with others in a peaceful way.
21. Everyone has the right to take part in the government of their country, which should be chosen through free and fair elections.
22. Everyone has the right to social security.
23. Everyone has the right to work for a fair wage in a safe environment and to join a trade union.
24. Everyone has the right to rest and leisure.
25. Everyone has the right to a standard of living adequate for the health and well-being of himself and of his family, including food, clothing, housing, medical care and necessary social services.
26. Everyone has the right to education, including free primary education.

27. Everyone has the right to share in their community's cultural life.
28. Everyone is entitled to a social and international order in which the rights and freedoms in this Declaration can be fully realised.
29. Everyone must respect the rights of others, the community and public property.
30. No-one has the right to take away any of the rights in this Declaration.

European Convention on Human Rights (abbreviated version)

Article 2: Everyone has the right to life.
Article 3: Everyone has the right not to be tortured or treated in an inhuman or degrading way.
Article 4: Everyone has the right to be free from slavery or forced labour.
Article 5: Everyone has the right to liberty.
Article 6: Everyone has the right to a fair trial.
Article 7: Only the courts can punish someone for a crime.
Article 8: Everyone has the right to have their private life and family life respected.
Article 9: Everyone has the right to their own beliefs or opinions.
Article 10: Everyone has the right express their own opinion.
Article 11: Everyone has the right to join groups or meet with others.
Article 12: Everyone has the right to marry and have a family.
Article 13: Everyone has the right to an effective remedy.
Article 14: Everyone has the right not be discriminated against in relation to the rights contained in the Convention.

Protocol 1

Article 1: Protection of property.
Article 2: Right to education.
Article 3: Right to free elections.

Protocol 4

Article 1: No imprisonment for debt; Freedom of movement; No expulsion of nationals.
Protocol 6 (and 13)
Abolition of the death penalty.

Protocol 7

Includes: Safeguards for expulsion of nationals; Right to appeal; Compensation for wrongful conviction; Right not to be tried or punished twice; Equality between spouses.

Protocol 12

General prohibition of discrimination (not just "in relation to the other rights …").

Appendix 2: Testimonies

Ilona Lendvai – deported with her family to Camp Csillagerőd

Ilona Lendvai was born in 1938 into a family of sedentary Roma in Tüskevár in Western Hungary. In 1944 she was deported with her whole family to the Csillagerőd fortification of Komárom.

"We lived in Tüskevár. We were four children. I was six when we lost our father. The Germans deported him in 1944. The Roma called him Csuri, but his name was István Lendvai. From there, from Komárom, they took my father, my grandfathers and my uncles to Germany and Dachau. Only an uncle on my mother's side came back three years later. Since then the poor man has also died. Only he came back from all these families.

My father worked at a butcher's with his younger and older brothers. He was a driver... . In those times my grandfather had horses. Because, you know, all the Roma like us had horses. He travelled to markets, sold them, bought some others; he traded them. He had a big family, five daughters and three sons, thank God. Our family was big. In those times we lived in style, not like the other Roma who did not have anything.

They took us in October. For eight months. In the bar, a peasant, a friend of my uncle told him, 'Flee, old friend, because they will take you!' But we did not have time to run away, because that night they came for us. They pulled us out of the beds. My mother had barely time to dress, and they took us away. There were some Hungarians who defended us. One was transported because he defended the Roma.

He told them not to hurt the Roma, because they were working Roma. He told them to leave the Roma alone. So they took him, and he did not ever come back again."

With her whole family, Ilona was first taken to a regional camp in the provincial town of Devecser and from there finally to Komárom, from where all her male relatives were brought to Dachau.

"We arrived in Komárom. They drove us like sheep. They brought corn stalks and spread them out on the ground, so our place was relatively clean, compared to what was there... .

I had not seen so many corpses before in my life. There every day we saw a crowd of corpses, children and elderly people as well. Lots of them starved to death. Those who talked back were shot in the head or beaten to death right away. They beat them until they died. But there were some guards who felt sorry for the people. Sometimes they would throw us a piece of bread or they would not talk so rudely to us.

We could only go out into the courtyard when they distributed the food. The resourceful among us went there two or three times. They did not notice it because there were so many people. One family was given half a kilogram of bread. And coffee in the morning. Cabbage had been cut into pieces and boiled in salty water.

That was what they gave us, and carrots boiled the same way in salty water. And sometimes a few potatoes.

Some [Roma] brought food with them. They let them take it in. One of them had a pack of flour, the other had meat and fat. They had carried it with them on their backs. Once my aunt said to one of them, 'Please give me some grease!' But he did not, he put it aside. The people did not want to give food to one another.

I was the oldest child in the family. I had three smaller brothers and sisters. Once when I went out to get some food, the other Gypsies took the bread out of my hand. I said, 'I hope God will not save you and you will die from it, die from that bread, if you are able to steal something, that I wanted to give to my little brothers or sisters.' But he took it. And whether you believe it or not, he died, the one who took it from me.

The resourceful ones could feel good. The women went to the kitchen to help out cleaning potatoes, vegetables, carrots and to steal something so we could eat. My aunt even managed to get some grease. They prepared a soup for us. That was something! If they had caught them stealing, they would have beaten them to death ... .

There was a woman from Nyarad and another one, who slept with the guards. Their lives were a little better. I am angry with them because I saw them hitting the others. They felt they were above us, that they could give orders. And they survived."

Ilona Lendvai survived, returned to her home town, married and eventually raised five children. But she never forgot her poor father. Her father had served as a soldier in the First World War, which he survived against all odds, and died in Dachau ... .

"The men were there for nine days. Then they separated us. Only the mothers with families and the children could stay together. Seven men. Father, my grandfathers and their sons. Only my uncle came home. They took them to Germany. That was the last time we saw them. My mother saved two girls who were our relatives. She gave them my sisters, and they pretended the children were theirs, so they survived. Nobody checked us. My dear father. They took him away and we never saw him again. My uncle saw him dead in Dachau. He recognised the body of my father. He said they were killed in gas chambers. They pushed them into the gas chambers and showered gas upon them. And the dead they put between rows of wood, one layer of corpses and one layer of wood and then they lit them. They burned the poor ones. Unfortunately this is what happened. My uncle told me many times, I saw what happened to your father!"

János Bársony and Ágnes Daróczi (Eds.), Pharrajimos: The Fate of the Roma during the Holocaust, New York, Amsterdam, Brussels, 2008; Gábor Bernáth (Ed.), Roma Holocaust –Recollections of survivors, Budapest, 2001

Anuța Branzan – deported with her family to Transnistria

Anuța Branzan was eight years old in 1942, living with her parents and three sisters in a provincial town in southern Romania. She describes her family as poor, tight-knit, and happy. In their two-room house with dirt floors, Anuța remembers her father Radu doting on the children between his work as a shoemaker and part-time musician. Her mother Constantina was a housewife, and was close to her extended family who lived nearby and frequently helped out with the girls. The second daughter in the family, Anuța had completed first grade and was looking forward to school starting again that September when the police came unexpectedly and announced their "resettlement".... . The family was deported the very same day, and placed temporarily in a soccer stadium in a nearby city. Days later, shoved into cattle cars, they were sent with some 13,000 other settled Roma to Transnistria, where nomadic Roma had already arrived months before.

"We did not have contact [with the villagers]. We were kept under armed guard. We weren't even allowed to go get some water. If the water came they would knock at the gate, yell from the street to come out with your bucket, your pitcher, cups, whatever you had to get water from the wagon. If you didn't have anything [to put it in] or if you couldn't go out because you were sick, you suffered. You did not even have water to wet your mouth, not even a cup of water. We were not even allowed to go to water. Nothing. The [villagers] were not allowed to come to us and we were not allowed to go to them. They tortured us to kill us.

[Guards] gave us a little bit of food or none at all. We were like sick cows, closed in. No food. For a while they brought us some grains like for the cows, a can filled with grains, but not more than [for] two or three months. They gave us barley like we were cows. A Russian would come and my father would go out [to meet him], to give us a can filled with barley. Who could eat barley? Who? Like we were horses, so they gave us barley? And then they didn't give us anything anymore. Absolutely nothing. And there was no doctor there with us. No medication. Absolutely nothing ... .

Luckily, an old Russian would bring us food. He was the owner of the house where we stayed. They were forced out, too. He would bring something from time to time. My father gave him the best of what we had. The sheets my mother made, good clothes, whatever he had. My mother and father gave the Russian man earrings, bracelets, whatever they had, to get some potatoes.

But [the Russian] would tell us he cannot give us more, that he barely had enough for his family, because they had rations, too. The army had carried off [the harvest] and they were not the masters there anymore. We got some milk, corn, and ate it like cows, because we did not have what to cook it in, or how to boil it.

'With what can I cook this corn, these potatoes?' My father asked the Russian. 'I can't come [with fire wood],' he said, 'because I am afraid the gendarmes would catch me and they'll shoot me. I'll give you a hoe to carve pieces from that tree in the yard to make a bit of fire.'

We made a little fire and steam, to cook a little. [The food] was mostly raw. But we could eat it.

To think, I wasn't even eight or nine years old, what could I do? As long as [my parents] were alive I didn't suffer very much. My mother gave us her food. My father sold everything we had. He sold most of the clothes, even some that were ripped. So we wore like a sweater. The clothes became too little so my father sold them. [Later] in the summer we foraged some greens – grass, roots to eat. We did not even have water to drink. Thin. Wretched … .

The powers from above must have kept us alive. We were without food, without water. Like animals in the wild. You waited – maybe you would die. You expected only to die. You did not expect any joy. Your day to die, that's all you waited for there."

From Michelle Kelso's paper "Recognizing the Roma: a study of the Holocaust as viewed in Romania"

Maria Peter – deported to Auschwitz

"We travelled for two and a half days. We reached Auschwitz in the middle of the night. My whole family was there: my parents, my brothers Eduard and Josef … and my three sisters Antonia, Josefina, and Katharine with their husbands and children … . They crowded us into the barracks. At dawn we got tea in enormous bowls. I drank my tea outside in front of the barracks and I saw – for the first time I saw something so terrible, and I will never forget the sight – a pile of naked bodies. The sight of the corpses terrified me so much that I went back inside the barracks … .

In Birkenau we all had to do slave labour. I worked on the building of the camp road, carrying heavy stones. My sister-in-law and her three children came down with typhus and died in the Krankenbau. They were the first members of our family to die in Auschwitz. Next, my sister Josefina's husband died of pneumonia which he picked up while doing hard labour in the camp. Then her oldest child died, and so one member of our family after another died. My sister Josefina Steinach had nine children and all but one of them died in the camp. To this day I cannot conceive of how the other eight survived until the beginning of August 1944, which is when they were all killed with gas. My sister could have lived. They wanted to send her to Ravensbrück before the liquidation of the Zigeunerlager. She refused on account of her children. She told the SS men that she was not leaving without her children. When the last transport was leaving Auschwitz, she died in the gas chamber … . My mother also stayed in Auschwitz. I did everything in my power for her, but my mother fell ill one day. She was running a high fever and the Blockaltester (block elder) announced that she had to go to the infirmary block. She had boils all over her body. They lanced those boils there and swabbed them with some kind of yellow fluid. She started seeing things and died several days later. My father and my sister Antonia also died in Auschwitz … .

I ended up in the barracks for children in Birkenau. That was the last barracks on the side nearer the entrance to Birkenau … . it was designated especially for children. I looked after the children during the day, and I served their dinner at noon. Those barracks were also where the orchestra rehearsed. I remember SS man Konig very well; after all, he gave me a flogging. He was present at almost every execution by shooting and during the arrival of new transports.

Konig gave me a flogging because I defended myself. It happened because of my sister Josefina's children. She didn't get food for them. I saw – and others saw it too – how Konig gave a crate full of food to the block nurse. All I wanted was for the children to have something to eat. So I complained. It was the day an SS inspection team came to the camp … . When the inspection was over, we went back to the blocks. Before much time had passed, the block supervisor appeared and called out my number. I had to go to the Schreibstube. Konig was waiting there with his legs in a wide stance, one hand in his pocket and the other holding a bullwhip that he was snapping against his high boots. I reported, giving my number. Then Konig came up to me and hit me in the face so hard I fell to the ground. Next he took me to another barracks. As far as I remember, it was the carpentry shop. There, on his orders, I had to undress and put on a pair of wet swimming trunks, which had been soaked in some kind of black liquid. I had to lie down on a trestle and count. I counted to seven – I remember it as if it happened just a moment ago – and I counted and counted, and then the first blows fell. I had to keep counting; by turns I counted and screamed in pain. I didn't think I was going to live through it. As he flogged me like that, he told me, 'You're going to die like an animal in my hands'. I'll remember those words till I die … ."

Quoted in Voices of Memory 7: Roma in Auschwitz. Slawomir Kapralski, Maria Martyniak, Joanna Talewicz-Kwiatkowska. Original source given in "Voices of Memory' is Memorial Book: The Gypsies at Auschwitz-Birkenau vol 2, Munich, London, New York, Paris, 1993

Appendix 3: Recognition and Commemorations of the Genocide in European Countries

Notes on the table:

- Data has been compiled from information officially submitted to CAHROM[5] by the member states of the Council of Europe.

- Explicit references to the Roma – either as victims during the Holocaust, as victims of a genocide, or otherwise – have been noted. Where no mention is made, the information was either not available or the Roma are not mentioned explicitly.

- All dates included have been officially recognised at national level unless otherwise noted. Events which take place at local level have mostly not been recorded in the table, even if these are regular features. **It is worth exploring this yourself** as there are many local or regional groups which organise their own events – particularly around 2 August.

Country	Roma officially mentioned or recognised as victims?	Commemoration days referring to Roma victims
Albania	Yes, included as one of victimised groups	**27 January**: Day of Commemoration for victims of the Holocaust. **10 December**: Schools observe a day devoted to "Good understanding and tolerant attitudes in schools". Holocaust victims remembered.
Andorra	No information	None
Armenia	Roma not included in official definition of Holocaust	**24 April**: National Genocide Memorial Day. This is a universal remembrance day with no particular reference to the Holocaust or Roma victims
Austria	Yes	**5 May**: Austrian Holocaust Day. Roma are explicitly included. The month of November is also used to commemorate the Roma Genocide.

Country	Roma officially mentioned or recognised as victims?	Commemoration days referring to Roma victims
Azerbaijan	No information	**27 January**: Day of the Victims of the Holocaust. **9 May**: Anniversary of the Victory over Fascism. Holocaust victims also remembered.
Belgium	No information	**27 January**: Holocaust Remembrance Day. **8 May**: Peace Day (includes reference to Holocaust victims).
Bosnia and Herzegovina	Not mentioned in definition of the Holocaust	**27 January**: Not officially designated as Memorial Day but is sometimes marked as such.
Bulgaria	No information	**10 March**: Day of the Holocaust and Rescue of the Bulgarian Jews.
Croatia	Yes, recognised together with Jews and Serbs as those who suffered most in the Second World War	Sunday closest to **22 April**: commemoration of breakout of prisoners from Camp III Ciglana Jasenovac. Official Roma delegation included.
Cyprus	No information	No information.
Czech Republic	Yes, officially recognised	**27 January**: International Holocaust Remembrance Day Parliamentary initiative to recognise. **7 March** for victims of Roma persecution. Various other days marked by Roma groups to commemorate particular events e.g. at Lety, Hodonin.
Denmark	No information	**27 January**: Auschwitz Day. Roma victims also remembered with other victim groups.

Country	Roma officially mentioned or recognised as victims?	Commemoration days referring to Roma victims
Estonia	All who suffered during the Second World War on the territory of Estonia are treated equally	**27 January**: Holocaust Remembrance Day. Roma always mentioned.
Finland	No information	**27 January**: Memorial Day for the Victims of Holocaust. Jewish victims remembered "as well as other victims".
France	Roma mentioned as victims	Sunday closest to **16 July**: National Day of Remembrance of the Victims of Racist and Antisemitic crimes. Remembrance activities also take place around **27 January**.
Georgia	Not mentioned explicitly[6]	No official commemoration day. Holocaust victims are included in commemoration events on **9 May**.
Germany	Genocide of the Sinti and Roma is recognised.	**27 January**: Day of Remembrance for all victims of the Holocaust. Near **16 December**: German Bundesrat annually remembers the Genocide of the Sinti and Roma in a commemorative speech. In November, a National Day of Mourning remembers "victims of the two World Wars and tyranny".
Greece	No mention in official definition of the Holocaust	**27 January**: Commemoration Day of the Greek Jewish Martyrs and Heroes of the Holocaust Holocaust Remembrance Day.
Hungary	Yes	**2 August**: Roma and Sinti Genocide Remembrance Day.
Iceland	No information	No plans to establish a Holocaust memorial day.
Ireland	No information	Sunday nearest to **27 January**: Holocaust Memorial Day. Designed to "cherish the memory of all of the victims of the Nazi Holocaust".

Country	Roma officially mentioned or recognised as victims?	Commemoration days referring to Roma victims
Italy	No official acknowledgment of the Genocide of the Roma	**27 January**: Day of Remembrance for those deported to concentration camps during the Second World War. Many Italian cities commemorate **8 April** as the International Day of the Roma.
Latvia	No information	**4 July**: Commemoration Day of Genocide against the Jews. Victims of the Holocaust are also remembered on **8 May**.
Liechtenstein	No	None.
Lithuania	No	**23 September**: National Holocaust Remembrance Day. Remembers all victims of the Holocaust.
Luxembourg	No	Sunday nearest to **10 October**: National Day of Remembrance. Remembers "all victims of war".
Malta	No information	No information.
Moldova	No information	Holocaust related events take place on **27 January**.
Monaco	No information	**27 January**: Day in Memory of the Shoah and for the Prevention of Crimes against Humanity.
Montenegro	Yes	**16 December**: Commemoration of the Roma Holocaust.
The Netherlands	Yes	**4 May** and **5 May**: National Remembrance Days. **27 January**: Holocaust Memorial Day. All three are days attended by representatives of Sinti and Roma.
Norway	Yes	**27 January**: International Holocaust Remembrance Day. Attendance and speeches by Roma representatives.

Country	Roma officially mentioned or recognised as victims?	Commemoration days referring to Roma victims
Poland	Yes	**2 August**: Roma and Sinti Genocide Remembrance Day. **27 January**: International Day of Commemoration in Memory of the Victims of the Holocaust. The remembrance event explicitly honours Roma victims. **19 April**: Day of Remembrance of Holocaust Victims and for Prevention of Crimes against Humanity – observed in all Polish schools (marks the Warsaw Ghetto uprising).
Portugal	No information	**27 January**: Holocaust Remembrance Day.
Romania	Yes	**9 October**: Holocaust Remembrance Day. Marks the date when the first Jews were deported to Transnistria. **27 January**: International Day of Commemoration in Memory of the Victims of the Holocaust.
Russian Federation	No [7]	**27 January** "has been commemorated by the offices of the President and Foreign Minister".
San Marino	No information	**27 January**: International Day of Commemoration in Memory of the Victims of the Holocaust.
Serbia	Yes	**16 December**: Day of Commemoration of the Roma and Sinti Genocide. **27 January**: Memorial Day dedicated to Holocaust victims. **22 April**: National Holocaust, Genocide and Victims of Fascism Remembrance Day.
Slovak Republic	Yes (?)	**2 August** is marked (Commemoration Day of the Genocide of the Roma) but has not been officially established at national level.
Slovenia	Not recognised as genocide	**27 January**: National Holocaust Remembrance Day.

Appendix 3: Recognition and Commemorations of the Genocide in European Countries

Country	Roma officially mentioned or recognised as victims?	Commemoration days referring to Roma victims
Spain	No information	**27 January**: Official Day for Holocaust Remembrance and Prevention of Crimes against Humanity. Roma and Sinti victims are honoured with others.
Sweden	No information	**27 January**: Holocaust Memorial Day. All victims of the Holocaust are commemorated.
Switzerland	No	**27 January**: International Day of Remembrance of the Holocaust.
"The former Yugoslav Republic of Macedonia"	No information	**12 March**: Holocaust Memorial Day (marks the deportation of Jews by Bulgarian opposition).
Turkey	No information	**27 January**: International Day of Commemoration in Memory of the Victims of the Holocaust.
Ukraine	Yes	**2 August**: National Roma and Sinti Genocide Remembrance Day. **27 January**: Holocaust Memorial Day. Honours all victims.
United Kingdom	No information	**27 January**: Holocaust Memorial Day. Roma included.

[5] Ad Hoc Committee of Experts on Roma Issues (Council of Europe). The data is taken from CAHROM 2013 (15).

[6] The Holocaust is defined as "the massive destruction of Jews during the German Nazi regime in 1939-1945". "Other victim groups" are apparently briefly mentioned.

[7] Although Roma / Sinti victims of the Holocaust are acknowledged, extermination of Roma during the Second World War is not officially recognised as genocide.

Appendix 4: Links to Online Resources

General resources on the Roma Genocide

- http://www.romasinti.eu

    This is a very useful online exhibition with general information about the treatment of the Roma during the Holocaust – for example, in different camps, on forced marches, in medical experiments, etc. Each section contains an image and brief accompanying text.

- http://www.romasintigenocide.eu

    This is an educational resource, "The Fate of European Roma and Sinti during the Holocaust". It contains numerous testimonies, images and background information, together with lesson plans.

- http://www.opusidea.eu/trr/index.php?PHPSESSID=b023c15efe7ac0868834cc28f4103aad

    A very comprehensive resource base organised under the Council of Europe in co-operation with OSCE-ODIHR. It contains numerous resources, including:

    » An interactive map of Europe showing what happened in different countries

    » Lists of reference materials on the Roma Genocide for different European countries

    » Lists of training materials on the Roma Genocide in different languages.

- The US Holocaust Memorial Museum (http://www.ushmm.org/wlc/en/article.php?ModuleId=10005219) and the Florida Center for Instructional Technology (http://fcit.usf.edu/holocaust/people/victroma.htm) also have pages on the Roma Genocide.

Testimonies

- Some (brief) testimonies from survivors are available at http://www.romasintigenocide.eu (together with images).

- http://www.hmd.org.uk/resources/stories/gypsy-roma-and-sinti-history-bock-family contains various narratives from members of the Bock family, a German-speaking Sinti family persecuted by the Nazis.

- "Memory needs a place" – a moving account of a visit to Auschwitz for a group of Roma by Sefedin Jonuz, a Roma who survived the war as a child in Skopje. http://www.errc.org/article/memory-needs-a-place/13

Images

Images of Roma victims of the Holocaust or which show the conditions of the camps and other hardships can be found at the following sites:

- http://www.historywiz.com/gypsyplague.htm - images and brief information about different aspects of the Genocide

- http://www.chgs.umn.edu/histories/victims/romaSinti - a selection of images relating to Roma discrimination through the ages. Contains a few which are specific to the Holocaust.

- http://www.annakari.com/portfolio/holocaust.html - a photo gallery of Polish Roma survivors, with brief information

- The sites listed under General Resources also contain various images.

Multimedia

The Council of Europe's resource base (listed above) contains an extensive filmography for different countries (and in different languages). This can be found at http://www.opusidea.eu/trr/index.php?PHPSESSID=b023c15efe7ac0868834cc28f4103aad

- The exile from Bessarabia is a documentary film which is available online at http://www.youtube.com/watch?v=9D1TeOyItHs. The film contains an account of the deportation of Roma to Bessarabia by the Romanian government, with archive photographs and interviews with survivors. Language: Romanian

General resources on Roma history / culture/ language, etc.

- Factsheets on Roma (Council of Europe co-production) http://romafacts.uni-graz.at/index.php.3

This site contains detailed factsheets on aspects of Roma history and identity. The history factsheets include an account of discrimination in Europe from the 14th century onwards, including discrimination in separate countries. They also have a section devoted to Roma treatment during the Holocaust.

- ROMBASE - http://ling.kfunigraz.ac.at/~rombase/index.html

Contains information on Roma history (including the Holocaust), politics, language, literature, etc. It also has a useful section on well-known Roma public figures, including writers, musicians, painters, activists, politicians, and so on.

Human rights

- *COMPASS* - The Council of Europe's manual on human rights education for youth leaders: http://www.coe.int/compass

Contains detailed advice on methodology, background material on human rights, a guide to taking action for young people, and numerous activities on different aspects of human rights. It also includes a section on Remembrance.

- *COMPASITO* – the Council of Europe's human rights education manual for use with younger children: http://www.eycb.coe.int/compasito

- *All Different – All Equal*: the Council of Europe's manual on racism and discrimination: http://www.coe.int/compass

- No Hate Speech Movement campaign http://www.nohatespeechmovement.org

- History teaching http://www.coe.int/t/dg4/education/historyteaching/default_en.asp

- Council of Europe Roma portal: http://www.coe.int/roma

   This contains numerous links to different initiatives and programmes under the Council of Europe, including:

   » Reference to Roma-related texts adopted by the Committee of Ministers, the Parliamentary Assembly, the Congress of Local and Regional Authorities and the European Commission against Racism and Intolerance (ECRI).

   » A database on Roma-related policies and good practices also directly accessible at http://goodpracticeroma.ppa.coe.int/en

   » Information about training and events organised by the Council of Europe

   » Information about the Dosta! campaign, also directly accessible in various languages at http://www.dosta.org

   » CAHROM website http://hub.coe.int/web/coe-portal/cahrom1

- The European Roma Rights Centre - http://www.errc.org

   The organisation works to defend Roma rights and the site contains extensive information on cases and violations.

- Fundamental Rights Agency – http://fra.europa.eu/en/theme/roma

   The FRA is an EU agency which works with EU bodies and government institutions to further human rights. They have a number of Roma initiatives listed on this website, including surveys on Roma rights, country data, policy documents and various projects supported by the agency.

Sales agents for publications of the Council of Europe
Agents de vente des publications du Conseil de l'Europe

BELGIUM/BELGIQUE
La Librairie Européenne -
The European Bookshop
Rue de l'Orme, 1
BE-1040 BRUXELLES
Tel.: +32 (0)2 231 04 35
Fax: +32 (0)2 735 08 60
E-mail: info@libeurop.eu
http://www.libeurop.be

Jean De Lannoy/DL Services
Avenue du Roi 202 Koningslaan
BE-1190 BRUXELLES
Tel.: +32 (0)2 538 43 08
Fax: +32 (0)2 538 08 41
E-mail: jean.de.lannoy@dl-servi.com
http://www.jean-de-lannoy.be

**BOSNIA AND HERZEGOVINA/
BOSNIE-HERZÉGOVINE**
Robert's Plus d.o.o.
Marka Maruliça 2/V
BA-71000 SARAJEVO
Tel.: + 387 33 640 818
Fax: + 387 33 640 818
E-mail: robertsplus@bih.net.ba

CANADA
Renouf Publishing Co. Ltd.
22-1010 Polytek Street
CDN-OTTAWA, ONT K1J 9J1
Tel.: +1 613 745 2665
Fax: +1 613 745 7660
Toll-Free Tel.: (866) 767-6766
E-mail: order.dept@renoufbooks.com
http://www.renoufbooks.com

CROATIA/CROATIE
Robert's Plus d.o.o.
Marasoviçeva 67
HR-21000 SPLIT
Tel.: + 385 21 315 800, 801, 802, 803
Fax: + 385 21 315 804
E-mail: robertsplus@robertsplus.hr

CZECH REPUBLIC/RÉPUBLIQUE TCHÈQUE
Suweco CZ, s.r.o.
Klecakova 347
CZ-180 21 PRAHA 9
Tel.: +420 2 424 59 204
Fax: +420 2 848 21 646
E-mail: import@suweco.cz
http://www.suweco.cz

DENMARK/DANEMARK
GAD
Vimmelskaftet 32
DK-1161 KØBENHAVN K
Tel.: +45 77 66 60 00
Fax: +45 77 66 60 01
E-mail: reception@gad.dk
http://www.gad.dk

FINLAND/FINLANDE
Akateeminen Kirjakauppa
PO Box 128
Keskuskatu 1
FI-00100 HELSINKI
Tel.: +358 (0)9 121 4430
Fax: +358 (0)9 121 4242
E-mail: akatilaus@akateeminen.com
http://www.akateeminen.com

FRANCE
Please contact directly /
Merci de contacter directement
Council of Europe Publishing
Editions du Conseil de l'Europe
FR-67075 STRASBOURG cedex
Tel.: +33 (0)3 88 41 25 81
Fax: +33 (0)3 88 41 39 10
E-mail: publishing@coe.int
http://book.coe.int

Librairie Kléber
1 rue des Francs-Bourgeois
FR-67000 STRASBOURG
Tel.: +33 (0)3 88 15 78 88
Fax: +33 (0)3 88 15 78 80
E-mail: librairie-kleber@coe.int
http://www.librairie-kleber.com

GREECE/GRÈCE
Librairie Kauffmann s.a.
Stadiou 28
GR-105 64 ATHINAI
Tel.: +30 210 32 55 321
Fax.: +30 210 32 30 320
E-mail: ord@otenet.gr
http://www.kauffmann.gr

HUNGARY/HONGRIE
Euro Info Service
Pannónia u. 58.
PF. 1039
HU-1136 BUDAPEST
Tel.: +36 1 329 2170
Fax: +36 1 349 2053
E-mail: euroinfo@euroinfo.hu
http://www.euroinfo.hu

ITALY/ITALIE
Licosa SpA
Via Duca di Calabria, 1/1
IT-50125 FIRENZE
Tel.: +39 0556 483215
Fax: +39 0556 41257
E-mail: licosa@licosa.com
http://www.licosa.com

NORWAY/NORVÈGE
Akademika
Postboks 84 Blindern
NO-0314 OSLO
Tel.: +47 2 218 8100
Fax: +47 2 218 8103
E-mail: support@akademika.no
http://www.akademika.no

POLAND/POLOGNE
Ars Polona JSC
25 Obroncow Street
PL-03-933 WARSZAWA
Tel.: +48 (0)22 509 86 00
Fax: +48 (0)22 509 86 10
E-mail: arspolona@arspolona.com.pl
http://www.arspolona.com.pl

PORTUGAL
Marka Lda
Rua dos Correeiros 61-3
PT-1100-162 LISBOA
Tel: 351 21 3224040
Fax: 351 21 3224044
Web: www.marka.pt
E mail: apoio.clientes@marka.pt

**RUSSIAN FEDERATION/
FÉDÉRATION DE RUSSIE**
Ves Mir
17b, Butlerova.ul. - Office 338
RU-117342 MOSCOW
Tel.: +7 495 739 0971
Fax: +7 495 739 0971
E-mail: orders@vesmirbooks.ru
http://www.vesmirbooks.ru

SWITZERLAND/SUISSE
Planetis Sàrl
16 chemin des Pins
CH-1273 ARZIER
Tel.: +41 22 366 51 77
Fax: +41 22 366 51 78
E-mail: info@planetis.ch

TAIWAN
Tycoon Information Inc.
5th Floor, No. 500, Chang-Chun Road
Taipei, Taiwan
Tel.: 886-2-8712 8886
Fax: 886-2-8712 4747, 8712 4777
E-mail: info@tycoon-info.com.tw
orders@tycoon-info.com.tw

UNITED KINGDOM/ROYAUME-UNI
The Stationery Office Ltd
PO Box 29
GB-NORWICH NR3 1GN
Tel.: +44 (0)870 600 5522
Fax: +44 (0)870 600 5533
E-mail: book.enquiries@tso.co.uk
http://www.tsoshop.co.uk

**UNITED STATES and CANADA/
ÉTATS-UNIS et CANADA**
Manhattan Publishing Co
670 White Plains Road
USA-10583 SCARSDALE, NY
Tel: + 1 914 472 4650
Fax: +1 914 472 4316
E-mail: coe@manhattanpublishing.com
http://www.manhattanpublishing.com

Council of Europe Publishing/Editions du Conseil de l'Europe
FR-67075 STRASBOURG Cedex
Tel.: +33 (0)3 88 41 25 81 – Fax: +33 (0)3 88 41 39 10 – E-mail: publishing@coe.int – Website: http://book.coe.int